Khenpo Kyosang Rinpoche

Snow Lion

Meets Europe

Foreword by Don McIntosh

GERIZIM

Acknowledgements

My humble acknowledgements

to Valerie — who has inspired and supported me these past years;

to Christian Lauer, the current director of the college founded by Rinpoche — who has initiated the project;

to Sonja Wagner — who was very helpful in preparing this publication in many unseen ways;

to Sophie Chechine — who has created her work of graphic art representing the Tibetan snow lion for the new, revised edition of the book;

to Boris Grechin — who has sponsored this publication from his own funds;

and, last but not least, to Don McIntosh, the editor of this book — who is probably the most tactful, and at the same time most thoroughgoing, editor I have ever encountered.

Ludwig Roemer

Contents

Foreword

When I was initially approached by the good people at Je Tsongkapay Ling, a Buddhist college in the U.K., about publishing a book of teachings from a Buddhist leader, I wasn't sure what to say.

I am a Christian, and a fairly conservative Christian at that. My faith in Jesus is like that of the apostles, in that I believe 'there is no other name under heaven…by which one must be saved' (Acts 4:12). I am not even optimistic or broad-minded enough to be a Christian ecumenicist, let alone a religious universalist. So the idea of publishing material from a non-Christian religious perspective seemed inconsistent with my convictions and calling.

Yet when I looked it over the material itself appeared largely unobjectionable and even illuminating. As Editor of Gerizim Publishing, then, I decided that we would be happy to publish the book — but on the condition that I had an opportunity to say a few words about it myself in the front matter. When I suggested, therefore, the possibility of writing a Foreword to the book from a Christian perspective, I was pleasantly surprised that the staff at the college were happy to oblige. (I should add that it was a genuine pleasure working with two members of that staff in particular, Ludwig Roemer and Sonja Wagner, whom I have come to regard as friends.)

Addressed to a European audience, *Snow Lion Meets Europe* is essentially a series of sermons/lectures on the state of Western culture by a respected (and recently deceased) Buddhist monk, Khenpo Kyosang Rinpoche. Going into writing this, I had in mind the basic idea of politely but uncompromisingly defending the integrity of the Christian faith. That is, I was expecting my faith to be frequently challenged and undermined, if not openly attacked. Instead, I was greeted with an insightful, mostly fair-minded analysis, not only of the state of Western culture generally, but in many places of Christianity in particular. That's not to say that there are no issues that I believe need to be answered from a Christian perspective. There are, and as readers will see I have tried to answer them.

For the most part, though, Rinpoche's critique is reserved for Western civilization generally rather than the Christian religion particularly. For example, in the opening chapter on 'Consumers,' he says: 'You believe that every labour brings suffering and that leisure always makes one happy. At the same time you regard laboriousness as one of the main human virtues.' Point taken! This love-hate relationship with work admittedly creates considerable anxiety and tension in our culture. With vacations and weekends we try to experience the leisure that promises joy, but we can't, because our work ethic continually reminds us that we should be increasing our productivity instead. So at work we long to relax, and while trying to relax we're itching to work.

For another example, Rinpoche addresses the simplicity and value of little things, which unfortunately get lost, even trampled upon, in the ongoing consumeristic pursuit of leisure. In an age marked by the 'ease' (or *annoyance*, depending on perspective) of, 'autocorrect' text formatting, targeted advertising, virtually unlimited television viewing options, and the like, Rinpoche speaks of a book created with woodcuts: 'Modern machines can print a book so that you do not need to copy it by hand or to cut printing patterns from wood anymore. However, if cutting your printing patterns took you a whole year you surely will remember the book you have produced this way. You will value it.' (As an editor who necessarily puts much work into the production of books, I say to that: 'Amen.')

The lesson? What's easily accessible or producible will not be considered valuable; yet we remain positively *addicted* to the ease which devalues our lives nonetheless. (One almost fears we are on the verge of living out the movie plot of *The Matrix*, with the difference being that now we are plugging ourselves into an artificial computer-generated world willingly and even eagerly.) The old texts to which Rinpoche alludes were at one time learned by heart; now, of course, they are simply stored on the Internet. So he asks: 'Do you have any knowledge left in your head, though, if you store it on the web?' In this he calls subtle attention to what has become obvious to many of us: that the world was actually a much more interesting place *before* the Internet. There was a time when my family and I could take a trip to a state park, for example, where part of the fun was using a map to navigate and anticipating what our destination might look like when we got there. Now, of course, a GPS directs our every move, and Google Earth photos reveal everything we might want to see beforehand, from every possible angle. I remember many years ago having a dispute with a college roommate, Forrest, about who played the role of Alan Shepard in *The Right Stuff*. I was *certain* it was David Carradine, while Forrest, though not sure exactly who it was, nonetheless swore that is was *not* David Carradine. As it happens Forrest was right; the actor was Scott Glenn. I was able to easily confirm that fact just now, thirty-five years later, by way of a Google search that took less than a minute – because now everyone knows everything instantaneously.

At turns and with terse wit, Rinpoche delves into topics such as democracy and government, women and relations among the sexes, youth and maturity, the power and influence of music, and the lies we tend to tell ourselves. To a present generation seemingly petrified of simple true observations, he says, 'Men are in reality neither better nor worse than women. They just *differ* from women.' Of course. When speaking of 'Worlds,' meaning the cultural-intellectual life spaces various individuals inhabit, Rinpoche calls attention to the hypocrisy — or more precisely, *blindness* — of a poor man who despises the rich, that is, until he stumbles upon good fortune; or of the rich man who despises the poor only until he himself falls unexpectedly into bankruptcy and debt. There are certain social horizons past which, evidently, we are simply unable to see. Rinpoche's insight seems to parallel, and perhaps even explain, the warning of Jesus: 'Judge not, that you be not judged.' Yet his is not simply a call to *tolerance*, for tolerance, he says, is reducible to *indifference*, which is clearly not compatible with love or compassion. This might further explain, he suggests, why neither the Buddha nor Christ were particularly tolerant.

While reading *Snow Lion*, I was occasionally saddened at the thought that the teachings of a Buddhist might at times be closer to the heart of Jesus than the often shallow and self-serving verbiage that passes for Christian teaching in the church today. I say that not to disparage the church — I am a member of the church, after all — but to encourage fellow Christians to forget about money, status and ambitions for a time, and take that time to pursue honest self-reflection and repentance. Some might object that a non-Christian has no place to reprove the church. But given the lesson of Jesus in the story of the Good Samaritan, it may be that nonbelievers yet have something to tell us. As the old saying goes, 'If you want to learn about water, don't ask a fish.' Sometimes a person standing outside the tradition can see it and speak to it more clearly than those who are most heavily involved and invested in it. (That comes close to the description of a *prophet* in the Bible.) So it is that Rinpoche speaks, for example, of consumerism in Christian life — of 'consuming' not only products and services, but sermons, confessions, and virtues, without the slightest strain or effort. In this he sounds like a Buddhist version of Dietrich Bonhoeffer, both men being equally contemptuous of the notion of 'cheap grace,' of happily accepting all the favor and blessings of God while refusing the cost of following him.

Does this mean that as a Christian I wholeheartedly embrace or endorse Rinpoche's teachings? No. As a Christian I cannot. I cannot, for example accept his stated belief in *karma*, let alone his belief that the crucifixion of Jesus was a result of the cleansing of the Temple and thus a demonstration of how the law of karma operates. By all (Gospel) accounts, Jesus died quite voluntarily, in order to fulfill the Father's purpose – not because the law of karma caught up with him. Grace defies karma, even as it defines the gospel. Rinpoche says that 'no religion can lead a person to Liberation except through cultivating the six perfections.' But Jesus came to liberate precisely those who could not liberate themselves, whether by cultivation of the six perfections, or keeping the Law of Moses, or any other means.

Likewise I would have to take exception to Rinpoche's apparent suggestion that no single religion can be 'the universal good' for humanity, given the many exclusive self-declarations of Jesus as, for instance, 'the Light of the World.' An argument could be made that to believe in Jesus at all is to believe that he is the one and only Savior of humanity. In one place Rinpoche suggests that Jesus was impractical, going to the trouble of changing water into wine when he could have simply made the proper arrangements to stock the wedding hall with enough wine beforehand. Even if, as seems likely, Rinpoche was speaking with tongue-in-cheek to his overly pragmatic Western friends, the point remains that there was a 'method to the madness' with Jesus. John called the miracle at Cana and other miracles of Jesus 'signs,' because they were given not merely to meet the immediate practical need at hand, but to reveal that God himself was present in the event.

Despite all this I can say with some confidence that had I the opportunity of meeting Rinpoche, I would have liked him. Or, since it has often been said, justifiably, that the words captured in books continue to speak long after the departure of the speaker, I *do* like him. Rinpoche's highly distilled reflections on the Western mindset remind me of another late great observer of culture, Allan Bloom. Indeed, both Rinpoche and Bloom openly lamented the loss of great music, art and philosophy; both seemed saddened by the disappearance of hard-working, courageous heroes and the rise of shallow pop icons like Michael Jackson (or Justin Bieber, more recently) who appear to have replaced them; both were keenly aware of the generally degrading effects of feminism; both perceived the enervating effects of premature and unrestrained sexual activity upon young and old alike; and both understood the power of music to not only arouse but inflame the passions.

So there remains, I think, considerable and commendable wisdom in *Snow Lion Meets Europe*. But it's not the wisdom of deep, mystical, faraway abstractions, the sort of thing I honestly expected upon starting the book. Much to the contrary, Rinpoche mocks the kind of artsy, intellectual pretension that causes anxiety and confusion — and yet passes for wisdom for that very fact. *Beauty*, he argues, 'never fills you with disgust and boredom you feel while watching some films for the intellectual elite, the films that you falsely regard as true works of art.' Instead, he advocates a more diligent, grounded kind of wisdom, the kind that is willing to work, learn and be patient. A Christian cannot but appreciate this, along with some of the other important commonalities between our faith and the way of Buddhism: the call to love, self-sacrifice, and rigorous discipleship.

Finally, a note about style: As the editor of this edition of *Snow Lion Meets Europe*, I was tempted to go through and systematically correct and modify Rinpoche's work the way I would for any other writer or contributor. But most contributors are free to let me know what they think of my edits and 'push back' a bit where they disagree with the changes, before the book goes to press. Given that Rinpoche is no longer with us, and therefore unable to respond to my edits, I have taken a deliberately 'hands-off' approach and with relatively few exceptions left the original text intact. The result is a text that is perhaps not 100% grammatically, let alone politically, correct, but which (I hope) remains highly readable, reflects the personality of the man, and retains a certain regard for history in light of his passing.

Don McIntosh
Editor, Gerizim Publishing
San Antonio, Texas

A Few Words About How the Book Was Written

This book is, by its genre, a collection of religious sermons. However, its author, Khenpo Kyosang Rinpoche, who used to live in Europe for many years, never was a priest. He, the founder and the first director of the Je Tsongkapay Ling Buddhist College, was an outstanding Buddhist lama.

Rinpoche never wrote these sermons (in Buddhism, the word 'teachings' is more common). He delivered them orally on different occasions, and he never cared much whether his teachings would be recorded, or written down, or published as a book (he rather disliked the latter idea).

On these occasions, Rinpoche used to speak in his peculiar manner: in short abrupt sentences; rather ungrammatically and with a strong accent, but at a quick pace; with moderate gesticulation; looking around the audience with his keen eyes; in a mixture of English and German words; occasionally quoting an old Buddhist text, or a minor Austrian poet of the nineteenth century, or referring to a French comedy film. It was astonishing to learn how much he (unlike so many Tibetan Buddhist teachers) knew about the Western classical music or the Western classical literature. His tone was often humorous (more often serious, though), and his speech was sometimes interrupted by bursts of laughter. He could masterfully absorb the attention of his audience.

The teachings were recorded by your humble servant as carefully as I could. I couldn't help rephrasing some obscure phrases, omitting repetitions etc. In many cases I had to make a hard choice between two options: either to keep Rinpoche's original words and grammar or to paraphrase the sentence — and to regretfully see that *the zest is gone*. The text below is therefore not a literal recording of what Rinpoche said, but it is as close to the true essence of his teachings as was possible for me to write.

* * *

Rinpoche had a sincere and sympathetic interest in Christianity. His views on Christian tenets or, say, everyday parish activity may be naïve, dubious or, indeed, erroneous (from the Christian point of view, at least), but they never were condescending or hostile. He clearly saw Christianity as an alternative spiritual path to 'the Final Liberation,' as a community of practitioners, some of whom sincerely try to accomplish the most noble task of stopping each and every suffering on earth. This service to people's needs is a feature wanting in Buddhism, he observed regretfully.

However, it is clearly not Rinpoche's catechistic notes on Buddhism (much less on Christianity) that make this book worth reading. Rinpoche's conventional teachings on specifically Buddhist subjects (such as the *Vinaya,* the monastic code of behaviour) were very orthodox, but his way of looking at the contemporary reality of today was rather unique.

Unlike so many religious teachers, Rinpoche never hesitated to air the ideas that so many traditional followers of any major religion, confronted with the brave new world of today, probably share but seldom express. He was an *enfant terrible* of Tibetan Buddhism, the street boy of *The Emperor's New Clothes* by Hans Christian Andersen who, while observing the absurdities of political correctness, was never afraid to exclaim, 'The king is naked!' While being not the only subject of *Snow Lion Meets Europe,* this simple idea we are sometimes afraid to say out loud is probably the most important message of the book.

* * *

The first title of the book was *Teachings Beyond Tradition.* Rinpoche obviously disliked this title. He said that no one of his sermons went beyond orthodox Buddhist views. For him, the fierce defendant of traditional values as he was, the very idea of being 'not traditional' and even 'not quite orthodox' was probably disgusting. On the day I was painfully searching for the new title I suddenly came across the picture of *the Lion and the Unicorn* created by Sir John Tenniel as an illustration to the famous fairytale by Lewis Carroll. I showed this picture to Rinpoche, and he laughed heartily. 'This lion represents Europe of today,' he said. This is how the present title (and the frontispiece picture) appeared. Of course, most readers will also recognise the 'snow lion' from Tibetan Buddhist tradition who symbolises strength and wisdom. I would invite the reader to see the two lions as symbols of their corresponding cultures, and the whole picture as West and East trying to understand each other — rather than oppose each other with hostility.

'May all sentient beings be happy.'

Ludwig Roemer

Consumers

Sometimes we have to talk about worldly matters. There are in fact no 'religious' and 'worldly' matters existing separately from each other. The law of karma is valid anywhere, no matter if one is religious or not. Why believe that only monks and priests obey this law? Everyone who draws a distinct line between religious truths and 'worldly' matters is mistaken. In doing so one believes that religion is not a 'real thing,' that it is of no use for the world we live in. Only the modern Western society regards religion as 'an abstract thing.' During the Middle Ages you Westerners used to have a different opinion. The medieval Christianity was making enormous efforts to erect the Kingdom of Heaven on earth. Its efforts failed.[1] Yet they were made. Crowds of people from the West, the poor and the rich, left everything they had and went to Jerusalem, to 'liberate the holy town of Jesus from pagans,' having no other more practical aim in view. When remembering your Crusades, how can you keep saying that religion is not capable of altering the world we live in? However, all the changes any religion is capable of depend on human mind. Things for us are exactly what we believe they them to be. If we believe in religion being a force that changes the world, it becomes powerful. If we believe in religion being 'an abstract thing,' it does become an abstract thing necessary only for scholars.

Right now most of you Western people regard religion as an abstraction created by scholars. That is why you distinguish between religion and 'the world.' You are surprised each time a religious professional begins to speak about 'the world,' about something he or she had never dealt with. In fact a person is either clever or not. One either knows the world or does not. There is only one world — which doesn't mean we know all of it. No

---

[1] A dubious statement — *L. R.*

'separate religious world' exists. A religious practitioner has to know the world, human emotions, men, and women better than anyone else does. One cannot be a world-knower *despite* one's own knowledge of religion. On the contrary, a religious person learns and understands the world *by the very means* of religion. If not, one's religion is useless.

I believe many of you regard Christianity as a useless teaching. This is why you study Buddhism. I think you are mistaken. The religion you call useless has been existing for two millennia. I have ever wanted to study Christianity thoroughly, to distinguish pseudo-Christian lies from Christian truths. I believe there is much truth in this religion. Yet [some] people who call themselves followers of Jesus fiercely defend their lies. Why, your society is built on those lies. I know little about Christianity. I am not competent enough to speak about this religion, and I honestly admit my ignorance. To speak about it, I had to be a Christian. Neither am I going to speak about Buddhism this time. In fact, I was going to speak about mistakes one clearly sees with the help of Buddhism.

About consumption.

We shall begin with the Teaching, though. You all know that the Noble Path consists of eight factors, being correct knowledge, correct thoughts, correct words, correct deeds, a correct way to earn money, correct efforts, correct attention, and correct concentration.[2] Why do I remind you of this? To show you that you cannot go any distance on this Path without your own efforts.

You cannot just press a button and start a machine of correct speech. Neither can you simply learn by heart the 'correct words' you need. Correct words do not exist independently

---

[2] Also referred to as (1) right view, (2) right resolve, (3) right speech, (4) right conduct, (5) right livelihood, (6) right effort, (7) right mindfulness, and (8) right samadhi — L. R.

from their context. Imagine that you tell your disciple he or she is lying. It is quite correct to say this if you want to cultivate the mind of your disciple, to tame him or her. However, if you say the same words to your ill mother they won't do much good even in case they are true. Correct words never exist by themselves, on their own, without concerning particular persons or referring to specific things. To speak correctly, you have to reflect on how helpful to others is what you are saying. It means that you have to make efforts within your own mind.

It is also true when regarding correct deeds, correct attention, correct concentration, or a correct way to earn money. Why do you believe that only one correct way of living exists? Even monkhood is not this only way. Imagine that only one male on earth has survived a catastrophe. If this only man then becomes a monk, humanity will cease to be. Moreover, even killing other people is not always a corrupt way of earning money. Each soldier is a professional killer, to say the truth. However, sometimes people have to fight with others and to kill them. Even the Buddha[3] in one of His former lives killed a murderer who was going to kill five hundred persons. In each case we must meditate, in each case we must recall our conscience, our understanding of Good and Evil first of all. If we do not have any, no saint and no Teaching can ever help us.

The Path to Liberation is conscious labour. There is conscious labour. There also is an opposite thing: consumption.

It was money that once gave birth to the idea of consumption. What is consumption? It is the state of mind which is characterised by a passive waiting for pleasure or pleasant sensations. Consumers always believe that they have a right to have these

---

[3] The word is capitalised if it stands for the Buddha Sakyamuni, and left in lower case when it means 'a buddha' — L. R.

sensations. Why, they paid for them with their own money that they had earned before by their hard work.

The idea first appeared among *vaishyas*, or merchants. Other *varnas*, other social strata have their own leading forces. They are inspired, for instance, by the idea of service to the people, as priests, by honour, as warriors, or simply by love. As long as the idea of consumption stays within the third *varna*, it does not do much harm.

The trouble begins when this idea becomes attractive for other strata, when it enslaves people of science, art, and religion.

Let us begin with science.

When comparing your schools with the monastic school I once attended I clearly see that your Western education now has become so 'sugary' as it has never been before.

Some centuries ago, even Western students had to learn texts by heart. Now they have their computers and the Internet. The Internet is a great invention. Do you still have any knowledge left in your head, though, if you store it on the web?

Some decades ago, boys and girls studied separately. Now they are in one classroom.

Some centuries ago, you had no educational supplies but books, no other teaching methods except lectures and debates. Now there are films, games, and what else you can imagine.

In short, now you do everything for students' pleasure, everything to lessen students' efforts. This educational trend is 'democratic'. You should realise, though, that school, as a source of pleasure, will never be capable of competing with alcohol, drugs, and sex. Your school students realise it very well.

The very idea of general education is false. Why, you would never force someone who does not want to be a monk to take his vows. A person, forced to be a monk, is of no use for any monastery. However, you produce in big numbers your scholars, persons who are out of touch both with real and with religious life. In doing so you make a lot of people unhappy.

The image of school students who just enjoy their studies, simply have fun and make no efforts would never enter your head without the idea of consumption. You believe that knowledge can be consumed, both by children and by adults.

Adults who keep studying and cognising the world are called scholars or scientists. Your science, too, is now characterised by consumption.

You believe that you may use your science to get as much pleasure as you can endure. Scientists invent clever machines for washing your linen, printing your books, or getting you to any place of the world with an unbelievable speed. Your personal efforts are not necessary now.

You see, the matter is not as easy as you think. Despite your going to another country by airplane you mentally stay in your own world, because you despise foreign cultures. Washing machines and printed books are surely a capital thing. Modern machines can print a book so that you do not need to copy it by hand or to cut printing patterns from wood anymore. However, if cutting your printing patterns took you a whole year you surely will remember the book you have produced this way. You will value it. Xylographic books are very precious. That is why no-one will print a worthless book by means of woodblocks. I cannot imagine a xylographic *Cosmopolitan*. Much less a xylographic *Playboy*. A huge amount of work needed to cut woodblocks is not worth the small value of a tabloid. Today, you can find on the web any book you want to get. Even audio books exist, so that you don't need to turn over the pages. Getting a book and reading it requires almost no efforts now. This is why books become less and less valuable. Once you asked me why I don't want to write a book.[4] Here is the reason. Understanding an oral teaching requires a lot of personal efforts. Anyone who wants to get real knowledge has to make efforts. Education without any efforts is worthless. Something you easily learn you easily forget.

Now let us deal with art. Books differ from one another. Besides nonfiction books, there also are fiction books, written by great authors. There is music, created by great composers. Some fiction books and music masterpieces belong to the world cultural heritage.

How do you Westerners see your great works of art, though? Some of you regard them as things that produce pleasant sensations without any efforts of yours. To say it in other words, you *consume* your art. In case one simply wants to consume works of literature and music, one surely prefers Michael Jackson to Beethoven. I do not mean that music by Michael Jackson[5] and Beethoven is equally pleasant. Beethoven's music can arouse in your mind an intense feeling of happiness. However, you need much less effort to listen to the music by Michael Jackson. You can simply relax and get pleasure from the latter. You do believe that you have any right to get your pleasure. Why, you paid your own money for a CD by Michael Jackson. A CD of Beethoven' Ninth has its price, too. So you wonder why you should make personal efforts, why you should 'work' in your spare time. It was hard to earn money for this purchase as it was! Now, instead of getting your pleasure, you have to work again. Is it clear now why some of you dislike your classical composers?

---

[4] *Snow Lion Meets Europe* was actually never *written* by Rinpoche, it is just a thorough and slightly edited recording of his oral teachings — *L. R.*

[5] This example clearly shows that Rinpoche was not very familiar with contemporary music trends — *L. R.*

I have just mentioned one of the main lies your society is built upon. You believe that every labour brings suffering and that leisure always makes one happy. At the same time, you regard laboriousness as one of the main human virtues. This is why you suffer from your 'religion' or from what you believe it is. Just consider: if leisure always makes one happy, some prisoners ought to be the happiest persons on earth. It was school that gave you the false idea of labour as suffering. At your schools, you performed difficult and sometimes senseless tasks. At your schools, your heads were stuffed with dead words. Why be surprised that some of you now detest any labour? The fact is that you want to consume your books, your films, and your music.

Some of you seriously believe that Michael Jackson is at the same level as Beethoven or, at least, that both are 'musicians.' These persons regard your modern music as an alternative to your old one. I am sorry, but it makes me think about idiots. Americans call their idiots 'persons with alternative talents.' Be honest. If an idiot has an alternative talent a normal person lacks then your idiots must teach children. Why, to cultivate children's alternative talents. I won't be much surprised if something like this happens at your schools in some decades.[6]

One can *consume* art. One also can *cultivate* one's own mind. One can do it by means of art. Here you make a fatal mistake again. You have persuaded yourselves that every labour is hard and brings suffering. So you believe that every serious work of art is hard to perceive, that its perception brings suffering. You can easily notice this idea when you watch European and American films. Many of them are fiction films of low quality, films for one evening. However, there are a small number of films one is hardly able to watch to the end, so loathsome they are. You call these films 'genuine works of art.' You could make no graver blunder.

____

[6] This prediction has to some extent come true — L. R.

The true art is always beautiful.

One German poet once said, 'Beauty is the beginning of horror we still can endure. We admire beauty, because it refused to destroy us.'[7] Beauty is similar to an invocation of a powerful *yidam*.[8] The presence of a powerful *yidam* fills your mind with simultaneous feeling of horror and delight. This horror is comprehensible, for too strong a feeling is able to destroy our minds. However, beauty never fills you with disgust and boredom you feel while watching some films for the intellectual elite, the films that you falsely regard as true works of art.

The true beauty is complicated. Compare a stone and a flower. Both are beautiful. And yet, the flower is much more complicated than the stone. Understanding of flower's beauty requires more efforts from you. A sonata by Beethoven is even more complicated than a flower. You cannot perceive the real beauty without your personal efforts, without cultivating your mind. A consumer never makes real efforts, though. The true beauty dies in case you regard works of art as objects of your consumption. I think it is dying right now. Consider that in the second half of the twentieth century no great European composer was born.[9] I may be mistaken, of course. There might be great composers

---

[7] Who, if I cried out, would hear me among the angels' hierarchies?
and even if one of them pressed me suddenly against his heart:
    I would be consumed in that overwhelming existence.
    For beauty is nothing but the beginning of terror, which we are still just able to endure,
    and we are so awed because it serenely disdains to annihilate us.
    Every angel is terrifying.
    From *The First Elegy* by Rainer Maria Rilke (who, in fact, was a Bohemian-Austrian poet), translated by Stephen Mitchell.
    It was your humble servant who first drew Rinpoche's attention to Rainer Maria Rilke and his *Duino Elegies* — L. R.
    [8] A Buddhist deity — L. R.
    [9] Another very dubious statement — L. R.

even now. However, their music is doomed to never reach a broad audience, never to be appreciated by many.

You surely tell me that it is not so bad. You say that you still have your concert halls where your old music is performed. To tell you the truth, some of your philharmonic concert halls seem to be places of consumption in the same way your shops are. You surely don't deny that visitors of a stadium attending a sportive event seldom do it in order to cultivate their moral virtues, do you? In a stadium, one just gets strong impressions while watching athletes who perform almost impossible tasks. It is pleasant to watch someone who is working hard. It requires no personal efforts. You see, a skilled musician, too, performs a very difficult task. You probably won't forgive him or her one single false note. Why, you have paid a huge sum of money for your ticket. This is why I believe that many so-called music-lovers are in fact consumers. These so-called music lovers never listen to your old music in their everyday life. You see, it is not music itself that attracts them. It is the skills and hard work of the musical performer. Besides, in a concert hall, a woman also has an opportunity to show her new dress to everyone. A man also has an opportunity, to show his new woman to everyone.[10]

The idea of consumption goes beyond education and art. You do believe that religion is a thing to consume either.

Let us begin with Christianity, with the faith most of you pretend to share. You go to church, listen to melodious prayers, listen to the sounds of organ, and get sweet sensations without many efforts of yours.

---

[10] I do hope that this does not sound misogynistic, as it surely was not intended to be — L. R.

Then a sermon follows. I have been reading some sermons of the most known Christian priests with much interest. Methinks[11] that some decades ago, Christian sermons used to be more critical. More burning. Now they are somewhat abstract. A priest tells you about things that ought to be there. Something about ideal Good. About sincere love for our neighbours. About love to Jesus. And so on. Gradually, you begin to believe that sincere love for your neighbours is very easy. Otherwise, you would be taught how to cultivate it. Eventually, you are convinced that you are capable of loving everyone, just because you are Christians, just because your faith makes you different from pagans. No-one would attempt to cross a big river without first learning how to swim. Yet no-one teaches others how to make children. Making children has never required much qualification. So you believe, at last, that love for everyone and even to Jesus is as easy as making children. This thought is pleasant. Moreover, the pleasure this thought arouses appears without any efforts of yours. You see, getting something without any efforts means consumption. This is why and how you consume a sermon.

Sometimes the idea that your life is wrong enters your head, though. You feel guilty. You go to church and confess your sins to a priest. The priest absolves them.[12] A completely false idea. How can a priest destroy your obstacles without your own personal efforts? Such a thing would contradict the law of karma. However, you believe your priest. 'Absolution of sins' sounds so lofty. This is how you consume a confession.

I know that long ago Christian priests used to give so-called penances to their parishioners. I mean penances similar to those we use in Sangha[13] for monks who transgress vows. Priests used to let the sinners read Christian purification mantras of some sort.

---

[11] I believe Rinpoche was aware of the difference between 'I think' and 'methinks'. I cannot say for certain, of course — L. R.

[12] To be sure, this vision of Christianity is to some extent very naïve — L. R.

[13] A Buddhist community — L. R.

This was very good of them. To be sure, purification practices do not suffice. You need other purification forces as well. The force of taking Refuge, for instance. Or a solemn promise never to do evil deeds any more. You may think this Buddhist view on Christianity is naïve. However, I believe that spiritual laws are essentially the same for all religions. How can you get rid of your obstacles if you do not promise to restrain from Evil? As for the Refuge, I do not specifically mean Refuge in the Buddha. Christians surely must take their Refuge in Jesus. Taking Refuge in Jesus and His Dharma[14] means that you trust in Jesus and in the Gospels more than in scientists, in your relatives, in your psychoanalyst, and so on. Now tell me: are there many people who do that?

Many of you get disappointed in Christianity, though. It seems to you, that this religion fails to guide you throughout your everyday life, that it doesn't help you live. To be honest, Jesus never promised to help you live. He promised you to bring you to the Kingdom of Heaven, which I think is the Christian name for the Final Liberation.[15] Any doctor is able to cure his or her patient only in case the patient takes the medicines prescribed and follows doctor's advice. I am not going to remind you of the words of the Gospel. You should know them better. In any case, you never follow them. So you grow disappointed in your doctor, although you never take the medications He ordered. You keep looking for another one. Half of Asia worships the Buddha, so you think, 'That is what I need.'

Buddhism is in fashion, besides. European priests are numerous, European *lamas*[16] are few in number. I must tell you that Christianity in China is in the same fashion. Today, you can find some Christians even in Lhasa. I even saw a Gospel translated into

---

[14] *Dharma* in Buddhism means 'cosmic law and order' and is also applied to the teachings of Buddha or, as here, of another religious teacher — *L. R.*

[15] Such parallels should be understood figuratively — *L. R.*

[16] Tibetan Buddhist priests — *L. R.*

Tibetan. It was quite the same ten centuries ago, when foreign teachers [in Tibet] were in fashion and no-one wanted Tibetan lamas. People never change.

You take Refuge in the Buddha without giving up your habit to consume, to enjoy effortless pleasures. I tell you how it ends.

You find a Buddhist lama and get a teaching from him. Not exactly *the* Teaching. Just a piece of it. Without listening to the end, you begin your practice. You are very impatient. You want to have results and pleasant sensations as soon as possible. In some time, having read several books, having listened to several lamas, you find a particular practice that seems to be more or less effective, a practice which seems to change your mind more quickly than other practices do. You don't realise yet that an effective practice seldom is the best one. Wine always changes our perceptions, for instance, yet it doesn't mean that wine is the very best liquid we can drink. It is also true for medications as well as for any medical treatment. You probably won't even notice what a skilled acupuncturist does to you. You don't understand it yet. You seldom ask a lama for a personal recommendation. You say it is so because lama's time is limited. To some extent, it is true. Nonetheless, there are resident lamas. However, you are not very keen on asking them for personal recommendations. Do you really believe that a lama will bite you or spit on you? I think you just feel ashamed of yourselves.

Why, since your childhood you have been told that you are similar to Jesus, that it would take you just several steps to enter the Kingdom of Heaven. Asking a lama or, indeed, a Christian priest for a personal recommendation will result in hearing unpleasant things about yourself who is said to enter the Heavenly Kingdom in short time. Yet some of you do ask us for personal recommendations. Then you go home and begin to perform the practice a lama advised to you. You keep doing it and see no results. Allow me to ask you, 'Why do you want to see them so soon?' No results can appear without much effort. You do not think of it. Instead of being patient, you say to yourself, 'The old foggy works unimaginatively. He doesn't take into account what a unique person I am.' It is exactly what you say, I know. So you go back to a practice you formerly had found on your own.

This practice brings some results: a feeling of warmth in your backbone, let us say, or a feeling of happiness, or some visions. So what do you do next? You begin to *consume* your practice. You have already learnt how to do it properly, so it does not require much effort from you now. Moreover, it brings pleasant sensations. This is exactly what you do it for.

Some of you stop here. Others experience an unexpected thing. They get troubles. The longer is their practice, the more serious are their troubles.

You never guess that this is exactly how it should be. Experiencing troubles is a good sign. Why, you have just begun your treatment, you have just started to expel poisons from your mind. You *should* have troubles. You simply need to endure them. Even enduring them for thirty years is too insignificant an effort when having in view the glorious fruit of the Final Liberation. However, you don't want to endure physical or mental pains for thirty years. Neither are you capable of enduring them for a single year. You give up your practice altogether. After that, some of you start searching for another practice. Others search for a new religion or get disappointed in any religion.

After all, most people are not religious practitioners. They deal neither with art nor with science. So why not consume? You believe you have a right to do it because you work hard and deserve a rest. Yet having consumed art, science, and religion, you start consuming love.

I mean both sexual and romantic love. You just want your love to pleasure you without any consequences, without working on mental and moral education of your children, for instance, without any children at all. The result is that your nations simply will cease to be; that in a century, only Arabs will inhabit Paris, only Turks will inhabit Berlin. Moreover, the result of worshipping sexual love is that your teenagers start their physical relations at the age of fifteen or sixteen,[17] and this damages their mind. They simply get silly. This is just what I mean.

You don't end up just having physical relations. You keep consuming romantic love. Why does it never enter your head that nothing in the Universe exists simply in order to pleasure you? Strong sexual feelings allow a child to be born. Strong romantic emotions provide a basis of creative work, of incorporating beauty. Consider [Johann Wolfgang von] Goethe, a German poet. Goethe could never have written his poems if he weren't permanently in love.[18] This is a characteristic feature of both European and Indian art. Our [Tibetan] art is not so splendid. We don't have glorious masterpieces of music, comparable to those of Beethoven. We hardly need them, though. A healthy person never needs to take strong medicines. I think it were the numerous spiritual illnesses of the West that gave birth to your old music which can be both powerful medicine and powerful poison for your mind. I regard some works of your art as the best thing your Western culture had ever created, as the true jewels of your civilisation. I am not going to say that these jewels are numerous. You see, you neglect even them. You want to consume your romantic love without any effort of yours. Imagine that every one of you would create a beautiful thing, inspired by one's romantic love. Europe would flourish, then. You probably believe that you do. Well, anyone may believe in anything: in communism, in fascism, or in the blossom of Europe.

---

[17] This sounds very outdated, I believe — *L. R.*
[18] Rinpoche probably mistakes Goethe for Heine — *L. R.*

There actually *is* an age at which a person is right to consume his or her romantic love without creating anything. It is youth. A teenager is not capable of producing great things for the sake of humanity. However, a romantic love changes his or her mind for the better. It is true for a teenager, not for an adult. A grown-up person, consuming romantic love, stays at the stage of a teenager. Consumption means getting pleasant sensation again and again. This is how a person becomes enslaved by one's own romantic feelings. These feelings become one's narcotics. Please pay attention to the fact that your popular culture is built on the cult of romantic love. What do you do with yourselves? Why do you need to transform yourselves into helpless children?

You probably will ask me what you should do. I do not know whether I am capable of giving you a good recommendation. Even the best recommendations never work. I will try, however. Here you have one.

Work on your mind. Give up consumption.

Robots

The Western society is built on machines. You live with them and even within them. And among them, too. Don't tell me that your environment has no impact on your mind. It surely does. We Tibetans are not very tender people. It is because our mountains never have been tender to us. To live in Tibet, one must be as strong as a yak[19]. Mountains are peaceful, though. You cannot fight with mountains in the same way you do it with the jungle. If you run too fast along a mountain path, you may fall off a rock and hurt yourself or die. That was why we have never been too aggressive: just strong, hard-working, somewhat reserved people. It was mountains that formed our national character.

It was forests that formed yours. I am far from criticising European culture. It used to be a beautiful one. Your music composers grew up in forests, so to speak. They always could go for a walk in a forest. There was something in your forests that inspired them. Now you have only a few forests left. You probably still have some, but of what use are they if they are too far from your big cities? Instead of them, you have your machines. Every kind of machines: cars, computers, mobile phones, lifts.

I don't say machines are bad. When I was a child I would be happy to get a washing machine. What is bad is that they now are your only environment. Your environment forms your character.

So some you finally become like human machines. Like robots.

---

[19] An ox-like mammal native to the Himalayas, Mongolia, Burma, and Tibet with dark, long, and silky hair, a horse-like tail, and a full, bushy mane — *L. R.*

You probably will say: 'Ah, this is an old comparison. An old and blurred metaphor. We knew it for ages.' You are mistaken. It's not a metaphor. It's simply reality. And even if you know it, so what? Are you proud of it? Some of you may even be. Do you find it all right?

Now you begin to disagree. You say: 'It surely is not worse. We are not robots. Some of us may be, but most of us are educated people, healthy both physically and mentally, free from your Asian complexes and your slavish devotion to idols and tyrants. Do you have any proofs that we are robots?'

Well, I have a lot of them.

A machine is driven by commands. It cannot perceive reality as it is. For a machine, it is too difficult. You just enter some commands, some words into it, and it reacts. Its reactions may be very sophisticated, very 'intelligent.' But *one* thing you cannot change, though: a machine always depends on words. And it always reacts in the same way. It never changes.

It is exactly how you live your social life.

When you meet a new person you first of all are eager to learn what he or she is. This means how he or she earns his or her money. You attempt to estimate one's value. You are grown to be great masters of this value estimation. You do it by the clothes one wears, by his or her manners, by his or her accent, and so on, and so on. A person is always wider than its profession, title, linguistic, or social habits. A commonplace, you say. But you refuse to look deeper despite the fact that it is a commonplace with you. You learn that this one is a scientist. That this one is a taxi-driver. Another one is a priest. This information is a 'command,' an 'input' according to which you react. At your schools or in your family you were told how to talk to scientists, taxi-drivers, and priests. You were pre-programmed, so to say. You may follow those programs or not, it doesn't matter. They are stuck in your mind. If you are not a truly religious person (and such persons are always few in number), you probably don't respect priests. You may criticise them, show them your lack of respect, and even abuse them. It matters nothing.

You behave like this *because* they are priests. So some of you automatically start to feel aversion towards a priest however good this priest may be. It is so because in your youth you were reprogrammed by atheistic ideas or by some 'gurus' of the Western world. And if not, something just went wrong with your machine. The computer of your mind caught a virus. It broke down under the heavy burden of lies your head was stuffed with. The program got a bug. So now you insult your priests and think yourselves to be 'free individuals.' Nothing of the sort. You are just acting in accordance with your new prejudice, with your new mental program. If you were unbiased enough you first of all would ask *who* a person is. Who he or she is, not what he or she does. You would try to learn him better instead of classifying him as this or that. If you did so you would learn that even a Catholic priest or a communist may be a good person. And that even a *Greenpeace* activist or a volunteer who helps aged people may be a bad one.

When I first arrived to Europe I was told that a large number of people show respect to me just because they respect me personally, as an individual. I was surprised to learn it, for I knew that most of my admirers obviously had no chance to get acquainted with me or to listen to my teachings before. Yet those who accompanied me attempted to persuade me that it was precisely so. Then, all of a sudden, hard times came. They said that I was a bad person, a false lama. I became ill and, to crown it all, had no money. Some good people helped me without asking much what I am. At that time I was nothing. An expat. An outsider. A beggar. And where were my former admirers? I still was the same I had been before. Only one thing had changed. The word.

The label. The command which prescribed how to perceive me, how to talk to me. A large number of people started to believe in this single word: a *false lama*.

Well: imagine that I really am one. Imagine that I am ignorant, stupid, and cruel. Why couldn't they see it at the first or at the second glance? Is it really *so* difficult, to notice one's cruelty and ignorance? It *is* difficult, however, if you are a robot. A robot always executes commands. It never perceives what really happens. It never gets its own way of thinking. You may think that it is only the old personal insult which now leads me to speak about your robotised mind. You are mistaken. You really are. I don't care much about myself. A monk can exist anywhere and must be ready to face his death anytime. I started to talk about this Western mental machinery after my first week in Europe, when I was listened to with much enthusiasm. I couldn't help speaking the truth. I wasn't going to preach 'sweet harmless Buddhism.' And I still am not going to be either 'sweet' or 'harmless'.

You probably disagree. You say that one cannot help judging others by their profession. You say that you have much more compassion and personal feelings for your nearest ones, for the people you love. At the first glance, it seems to be true. But in fact you have simply changed the label. You just put another label on your friends, relatives, and beloved ones. Having done so, you begin to call a former taxi driver or a former scientist your 'sweetheart.' But all your sweethearts are somehow similar. You treat them all in the same way. You act in accordance with the program 'partner' which was put into your mind, without analysing much what kind of a person your partner is. You allow them to have physical relations with you and to care for you; you become sentimental about them. You say, 'Oh, dear!' and so on. But in reality you have not much interest in them; neither do they have much interest in you. You don't study your partners. And you never really think who they are or what they are to you.

Someone has told you that a partner is a closest person to you, that now you have everything in common, that your partner shares all your ideas and convictions, and so probably do you. It is simply not true. He or she neither shall do it nor does it actually. *People differ*. Studying your partner would be of much use for you. You probably could learn something from him or her, as well as your partner could learn from you. Sympathy begins with understanding another person, with studying one. Having studied your partner, some of you would probably realise that you have little love for him or her. And even if you truly love someone, relations are not bound to be similar. Some of your beloved ones can help you, others need your help. One person can be hurt by your coarse words; another will be insulted if you are too gentle to him or to her. And so on. But you never distinguish them from one another. You act as robots executing the same program. As soon as the label 'partner' is put on a person, you share your bed with him or her, allow him or her to call you 'sweetheart,' and begin to regard one as another part of yourself.[20] Why, he or she has never been that before. Sooner or later, something goes wrong. The 'sweetheart' ceases to be sweet, tender, and sexy. Then you break up and probably start accusing another sex of your problems. After your first divorce you believe that men in general can never understand a woman. Not such a 'complex' one as you, at least. You believe that women can never understand a man. Surely not such a deep personality as you. Did you do anything in order to understand your first partner, though? I don't speak about everyone. I am glad to know that exceptions still exist. These exceptions will be in lesser numbers each year. They will be in lesser numbers because of the robotised mind which simply puts a label of a 'partner' on a person instead of studying one.

---

[20] Rinpoche may have missed the point here, as the modern marriage is characterised by emotional distance between spouses more and more often — *L. R.*

As for the much esteem you have for your nearest and dearest ones, I doubt of it. What is esteem? You respect a person if you are devoted to this person, if you find him or her superior to you, if you easily believe what the person says or at least appreciate his or her words, if you don't mind occasionally doing him or her small favours, if you do it sincerely and without any selfish interest. Don't mix up esteem with idolatry. In case you idolise someone you worship the person as a god. In case you esteem someone you see the person as a human being, you know why he or she deserves your respect. Western people have many idols. However, most of you are hardly capable of respecting anyone. You even fail to respect your parents. You seldom do what your parents say to you. You often argue with them. Why, you don't even respect your god, Jesus Christ. Do you really do much to please Him? Did you give up all you have, as He taught you to do? Did you ever give up any of your bad habits for His sake? Did you ever refuse to follow the smallest of your silly ideas, selfish desires, or addictions? Each religion starts from respect, from esteem, from devotion, not from philosophy. It also may be based on idolising, but then it simply degrades to fanaticism. How could we Tibetans, we poor folk master the immense difficulty of *Prajña Paramita*,[21] if we didn't have our true love and devotion to the Buddha, the Great Teacher? You see, you don't even respect your god and teacher which is, in my opinion, more than a god. The gods are many,[22] good teachers are rare. A machine is not capable of having religious feelings. Religion is something beyond words. But you do not want to go beyond.

This lack of respect combines with your lack of mental independence. Again you seem not to believe me. You believe that all of you have your own independent views. You believe you

---

[21] Literally, 'the Perfection of (Transcendent) Wisdom.' A body of very important sacred texts in Mahayana Buddhism — *L. R.*

[22] One has to bear in mind that, speaking of 'the gods', Rinpoche or any other teacher of Tibetan Buddhism refers to subordinate deities (it may be not fully wrong to call them 'angels'), not to the Supreme Reality which is one — *L. R.*

would never allow others to form your ideas and convictions. It is not true. You do argue with others, simply because some of you have a childish urge to argue with people. But only a few Westerners think their own thoughts. You are awfully afraid not to be original. Afraid to be like others. You awfully want to differ from the crowd.[23] Aiming for this you can do anything. You can even take Refuge in Triple Gems.[24] What does it matter? Taking Refuge or becoming a communist is just a way you re-program yourselves. You just stop executing the program called 'Christianity' and start executing the program called 'Buddhism.' But you are hardly able to execute the latter, because this Asian program requires much sincerity.[25]

You are as much afraid of thinking independently as of being said to be mediocre. Looking originally and thinking independently is not the same thing. Your thinking must always proceed in accordance with theories; you always must go the way other people go. If by any chance an idea which has never been there before enters your head you simply ignore it, because you have no tools to work on this idea. If a genius appears you immediately make one a laughingstock. You keep despising one, criticising one, and throwing mud at one until it turns out that this one is a real genius. A robot simply cannot have its own thoughts. Its independent thinking has nothing to rely on. Your thoughts are to rely on reality. But it's only words you stuff your head with.

Independent thinking is not always original. Throwing mud at priests or admiring homosexuals is, in your opinion, very

---

[23] This may seem confusing given the statements preceding, but I think it was Rinpoche's love for paradoxes speaking here: Westerners don't think their own thoughts, and *at the same time* they are afraid to admit it even to themselves and therefore pretend to be 'original' (not really). – L. R.

[24] 'Taking Refuge in Trimple Gems' is a Buddhist ceremony by which one is received into the Buddhist community, i. e. formally becomes a Buddhist — L. R.

[25] Which doesn't mean to say that being a true Christian doesn't require as much honesty — L. R.

original, because it is something that 'breaks traditions.'[26] Traditions might be of great use, though. On the contrary, studying the scriptures bores you immensely. And even if it doesn't you still are afraid of being called 'a traditionalist' which word for you sounds almost obscene. Yet someone who does think independently doesn't care what label is put on him or her.

Remember 1932, the year in which Adolf Hitler became the head of Germany.[27] As soon as he did it he declared that Germany should go back to its middle ages, should once again become a medieval empire. Hitler did think independently. He most probably was inspired by demonic powers, but a robot he wasn't. If someone declared such a thing now you would surely call the person mad. But Hitler you didn't. Quite the contrary: it had turned out that Germans had for ages been dreaming of it.[28] I don't blame you. I just want to show you how easily someone who has no true opinion of one's own is re-programmed.

You may think that there is a domain in which you still stay more or less spontaneous. I mean religion. A domain less robotised than other domains of your life. It may be so, may be not. I want to tell you a story I have never told before. Once I was very eager to learn what a Catholic mass looks like. So I went to a church. Not in a [Buddhist] monk's robe, of course. I believe I put on trousers and a shirt. There were laymen as well as nuns in the church. I listened to a sermon and to prayers. Then the communion followed. Having approached the priest I told him that a simple blessing would also do, and so he blessed me. I don't think that we Buddhists are allowed to take the communion. I don't know for certain, I may be wrong, after all. I went back to my

---

[26] What once used to be 'original' has obviously become a routine part of political discourse today — *L. R.*

[27] The year is wrong: Hitler was appointed as chancellor of Germany in 1933 — *L. R.*

[28] A very painful topic for every German. There was a lot of hesitation on whether to leave this paragraph intact or to leave it out from the text — *L. R.*

place. Then one of the nuns turned her head and gazed at me with disapproving eyes. I think she blamed me, because I broke common rules of conduct. I believe she even blamed the priest, for his simply giving me a blessing. How sorry I felt for this old nun!

Of course, one shouldn't be provocative during a ritual, I understand it very well. One never should hurt religious feelings of other people. You know, I shouldn't go to the mass in the very first place. But once I was there, I sincerely didn't mean to be provocative. And was it her feelings I hurt? Or was it just 'changing the code' the nun was angry with? Some of the few people of the West who still remain religious are terribly afraid of altering even the smallest detail in their religion. Do you remember that machines always work in the same way? If one single character in the code is changed the computer cannot execute the program. Well, we Tibetans are rather conservative in our rituals, too. However, we never perform rituals only for the sake of rituals. We don't mind altering our old rituals, we don't mind inventing new ones. We never believe that performing a ritual guarantees some spiritual achievements in the same way in which starting washing machine guarantees clean linen.[29] But you Western people are persuaded that a machine always performs its job. So you believe that prayers and communion will perform theirs. After your death, many of you will be very surprised to learn that they hadn't. Why, communion is not a machine. Neither is Jesus. If you perceived reality, not words, you would notice that performing rituals mechanically never changes anything. I just cannot realise how some of you can go to church for many years and be exactly as you had been. Only a robot can perform an activity for many years without being changed. Of what use is religion if it never changes anything in your mind?

---

[29] I do not think that faithful Christians believe in it either. Rinpoche's criticism is probably aimed at the mechanical churchgoers who exist in almost any religious community — L. R.

For a human being, religious activity like this is of no use. For a robot, it is useful, though. It puts into the human machine the old lies Western society is built on. It lets you feel like having performed your religious duties, so that you may remain a good robot. In a religion, no duty can ever exist. No-one is obliged to become better. No-one is obliged to achieve enlightenment. Yet some of you fancy that enlightenment will be achieved instantly after your death, that Jesus saves all of you from *samsara*,[30] that going to church and refraining from crimes is the only thing needed for it. This idea could appear only in a robotised mind, in a mind that deals with machines and believes the mysterious issue you call God[31] to work as a huge enterprise. I don't blame your priests. Even the best priest can change nothing when he preaches to machines.

And, last but not least, it's only practical benefit you think of. Why, no engine is created just to admire it. Each engine has to work. You Western people believe laboriousness to be the main human virtue. If it really were so, each engine would reach enlightenment much sooner than you. Did you ever see a saint machine? A human being can admire beauty. A robot cannot. It lacks the part of its mind which is responsible for perceiving beauty. And it is quite comprehensible, because beauty is perfectly useless for business matters. You will tell me that it is not so, that you still have your philharmonic societies, that your school students still study Shakespeare, Dante, Goethe, or any author belonging to your Western cultural heritage. Did you ever think how you deal with your cultural heritage? Most prag-

---

[30] A very puzzling mixture of Buddhist and Christian terms, as there obviously is no concept of samsara, or 'endless rebirths', in Christianity — *L. R.*

[31] While 'God' as a concept is normally avoided in Buddhism, many Buddhist scriptures state that the supreme all-pervading reality definitely exists. This reality is then described as *nirvana* ('something beyond evil'), *tathata* ('suchness') and so on — *L. R.*

matically. You were told by your schoolteachers that Goethe is 'a capital thing.'

You human machines are not capable of realising the beauty of his poetry by yourselves. However, you do believe in your teachers and scholars, and they keep praising Goethe. They do it almost mechanically, truth be told. They, too, are robotised. Nonetheless, they do their job; they reproduce the 'old faith in cultural treasures.' So you let Goethe, the poor man, be. But, as poetry cannot help annoying robots, as it is awfully boring to them, you attempt to make your Goethe 'comprehensible.' You simplify your great authors. You translate their works into the vulgar slang of your teenagers. You probably think that vulgarising them is better than deleting them from the syllabus altogether. That a half or even a third of 'a treasure' is better than nothing. You think of it in the same way you would calculate the efficiency of a machine. Well, if you reduce the capacity of a machine the machine is still useful. But if you 'reduce,' if you simplify *The Divine Comedy* it simply ceases to be. Its whole beauty is completely destroyed. This is a thing only a human being is able to realise, a fact a robot will ever fail to understand.

Please stop being robots! Only a human being can reach enlightenment. The Buddha said nothing about robots although He surely used to know some. Don't believe in words. Don't label people. Study them carefully, especially your nearest ones. Let each of your conversations with others be unique, don't follow the same pattern over and over again. Respect those who deserve to be respected. Don't let politicians or newsmakers guide you. At the same time, don't be afraid not to be original.[32] Give up your faith in robotised rituals which might be effective in a miraculous way, without any effort of your own mind. Develop

---

[32] This appears to be another paradox – encouraging 'unoriginality' in the context of a criticism of robotic behaviour. It's possible that Rinpoche here wanted to say that we should not be afraid of such 'unoriginal' or traditional things as having a (heterosexual) family, honest manual labour, or going to church on Sundays. – L. R.

your sense for beauty. Then you might get a chance to escape from the steel cage of samsara no robot can escape from. Why, a robot is made of steel. How can it go beyond the substance it is made of?

Democracy

There are things Western society does like in Buddhism. It is our calmness, our almost scientific analysis of mental processes, our lack of religious ecstasy and fanaticism. There are things it doesn't. It is our aristocracy, our deep respect and admiration towards religious teachers which is not democratic for your European taste — neither for American taste.

For you Western people, Democracy is a kind of god. You have two main gods: Jesus and Democracy. And these two gods have been rivalling with each other until now. Right now, at the beginning of the twenty-first century, the latter seems to have won this battle. Now you worship your Democracy much more than Jesus.

Making a god out of an abstract idea is not very good. Making a god out of a wrong idea is fatal for any nation.

Now you may ask me, 'Why is democracy a wrong idea?' Or maybe is it me who is wrong when thinking it to be wrong?

Well, it is quite easy to make people worship a god, and it is quite difficult to make them just a little bit cleverer. I will try, though.

You may know that there were four *varnas* in the old Indian society. The Brahmans, the Kshatriyas, the Vaishyas, and the Shudras. The priests, the managers, the merchants, and the servants. These four varnas exist in each human society. They are in your Western society, too. Don't think it to be so easy. You may count yourselves to priests because you are intelligent enough and have got a good education. But in fact most of you are Shudras. Why? Because you earn your money by serving others, by doing what other people want you to do. There *is* a difference between a brahman and a Shudra. The former always says what he wants to say, be it pleasant or not, and he earns his bread by it. The latter says what other people want him to say. Do you really think that your job at school, or in a newspaper, or in an office allows you to say something you really want to say? Don't be naïve. Naivety is a sin. For a Buddhist, at least.

There are different ages of humanity. Each age allows one of four varnas to prevail over others.

There was a time, many millennia ago, when priests prevailed. When no king could do anything against their will. This regime is called *theocracy*. Tibet was the only country that remained theocratic until the middle of the last century.[33] Until 1959.

Then times came when soldiers shot priests down, as they did in Tibet after the Chinese invasion,[34] and began to rule. It was not always as bad as in 1959. There had been kings who protected and helped their priests and monks, someone like the king Bimbisara, the Buddha's famous donor, or the glorious king Ashoka. In any case, a soldier cannot exist without an officer, and an officer cannot help being proud of his position. This regime is called *aristocracy*. Priests are bad managers, to be honest. They are always a sort of dreamers. Dreamers are very important for any culture. There is no religion and no art without them. But a dreamer will never run a state well enough. So there is a good reason why the Kshatriyas subdue the Brahmans. Warriors are courageous, strong, and clever. You cannot help being clever if your life depends on how clever you are. Don't forget that the Buddha was not a priest. He was a Kshatriya, a warrior. He wasn't a dreamer but for few moments of His glorious life. He was a perfect manager and scientist.

---

[33] This proves wrong when we consider theocracies in the Middle East etc. — L. R.

[34] The politically correct term for the events of 1959 is probably *Chinese Reunification* — L. R.

However, people get tired even of the best managers. The best are always few in number. Remember it well. No-one likes when the few rule over many. And there is almost no 'private life' during the age of aristocracy, too. A knight can be poor and proud. A tradesman never can. Besides, it is so annoying to be poor and proud, or poor and afraid of the proud! So a new revolution starts, and the kings lose their crowns. Now everybody wants to be a politician. Anyone has the opportunity to become a politician. Elections. Parliaments. Referendums. This regime is called democracy.

Now meditate. I don't mean meditation on the Buddha. Just meditate. Think of it. Analyse it.

Did it ever cross your mind that the good are always less in number than the bad? Just buy a dozen books, or films, or listen to a dozen lamas[35], and examine them by your own eyes and ears. People who are honest, courageous, and clever, are always in small numbers. Everyone cannot be clever and strong. This 'everyone' cannot help being mediocre. This is what the very essence of each democracy is: the power of mediocrity.

And then the Shudras, the servants or the slaves, come. The loudest ones. The rudest ones. It is slaves who have received the worst education or no education at all, that is why it is so. And then they start fighting for their rights of minority, like homosexuals or harlots do. And they triumph, at last. And they rule over three quarters of the modern society. And then they tyrannise over others, both in the economical and in the intellectual domain, because a former slave cannot help tyrannising over others, exactly in the way in which he was oppressed before. He has never learnt how to rule over others in a different manner.

---

[35] Tibetan Buddhist teachers — *L. R.*

The slaves want to rob you of your free will and to make you equal to them. Then it is democracy.

Democracy is built upon three concepts of the French revolution: Freedom, equality, and brotherhood.[36] These concepts seem to be very attractive. But in fact we are cheated by them.

First of all, a warrior or a priest is never equal to a slave. An elephant is not equal to a mouse. You will let an elephant starve by giving him the same amount of fodder as you would give to a mouse. But it is exactly what you Europeans do now.

And then freedom. It means freedom for the slaves. Freedom by itself is very good. But you must realise that slaves are the rudest ones. Kshatriyas are ruder than Brahmans, this is why the former subdue the latter. Vaishyas are ruder that Kshatriyas. And Shudras are the rudest folk. Which means, they are the strongest. If you keep both a sheep and a wolf in the same room, the wolf will kill the sheep. If you keep both Beethoven and Michael Jackson in the same room, the latter will annihilate Beethoven. Beethoven and Michael Jackson. An honest wife and a harlot. A heterosexual and a homosexual. 'Okay,' say you Western people, 'It is democracy and freedom, it is a natural *struggle for life*, and the sheep had had its right to fight. It was the sheep's fault that it never got teeth and claws,' you say. Allow me to dislike freedom of this kind, though. Jesus, your teacher, called Himself a shepherd, and a shepherd looks after his sheep. He does. You don't.

And brotherhood, finally. Regarding other people as your brothers is very good. But in fact there cannot be any brotherhood without compassion. How can you make a sheep believe in a wolf being its brother, or the other way around? Do you wish

---

36 The French Revolution was a period of far-reaching social upheaval in France beginning in 1789. 'Liberté, égalité, fraternité' (French for 'liberty, equality, fraternity') was the motto of the French revolution, first expressed by Maximilian Robespierre in 1790 — *L. R.*

your mother or your daughter to regard a lesbian or a harlot as her sister? Did you ask her whether *she* wants it? People most certainly can be united; most certainly can be brothers and sisters to each other. But this brotherhood starts by cultivating your *bodhicitta*, your sincere wish to achieve enlightenment for the sake of all living beings. By *Dharma.*[37] Slaves have not much Dharma. Dharma is of little use for them. They find it boring.

You seem not to agree with me. You say only Democracy can prevent a nation from being tyrannised.

Well, now think of your own history.

Do you remember Adolf Hitler, the leader of the German National Socialists? Do you remember that the fascists used to be a political party? That they participated in German parliament elections in 1932? That they *won* the elections? The Nazi party won the elections in 1932 in a democratic way. How dare you say now that your Democracy prevents bloody tyrants from seizing power?

His Holiness the Dalai Lama, unlike George W. Bush, never was elected. Which also means that his education never depended on mediocrities or slaves. And I must note that it was not His Holiness who invaded Iraq, right?

One year ago, my opinion was asked on whether a lama may be elected by members of a religious community from themselves and so become the community leader. A lama surely may be elected by the community. A 'lama' is just a word, a conventional term, there is no such thing as 'lama-ness' that exists independently and by its own force, somewhere in the air or in the

---

[37] *Dharma* is the Buddhist teaching, or any religious teaching in general (such expressions as 'the Christian dharma' are not uncommon in Tibetan) — *L. R.*

sky. You may elect any lama you want. But are you sure he or she will be a good one?

How can you become certain of it? There is only one way of finding a good lama: the feeling that you do get better by following his or her[38] recommendations. Getting better is never *very* easy. Therefore, lama's words never can be *very* pleasant to you. If you are wise enough to choose a man whose words are not very pleasant to you (something which seldom happens), then there is surely no harm in electing a lama by a democratic election. Democracy is neither bad nor good by itself, on its own. (The same is true for all things, as you know.) Democracy is good when people are good and bad when people are bad. Someone chooses the Buddha and someone else elects Hitler. This is how things are.

Nonetheless, a real lama, no matter appointed or elected, never can be a friend of the modern Democracy. What is a 'friend of the modern Democracy'? It is someone who lets the vice have its rights. Someone who says that homosexuals should be allowed to marry. Children should be allowed to disobey and neglect their parents. Rebels should be allowed to shoot at soldiers of the regular army. Students of theology should be allowed not to read the Tipitaka,[39] the Quran, or the Bible, simply because they dislike it. Erotic maniacs should be allowed to produce films. Perversity and ingratitude, hatred, ignorance, and lust are allowed and welcome in a democratic society, because everyone 'should be free and enjoy his or her freedom.' But this freedom results in the strongest slavery, when the three roots of evil become your tyrants and you their slave.

A lama is not a person who is tolerant towards hatred, ignorance, or lust. He or she is someone who cures them. Someone

---

[38] Female Buddhist lamas exist, however rare they are — L. R.

[39] A collection of early Buddhist sutras — L. R.

who forbids what is unwholesome. So he or she is easily said to be an 'enemy of Democracy.' *Tant pis,*[40] as you Frenchmen say. So much the worse. So much the worse for Democracy.

I am neither a politician nor a person engaged in politics. A monk cannot be one. So why so many words about Democracy? Because it has a huge impact on both the contemporary education system and the religious life of the West, not just on your politics.

Imagine that you are a teacher. Imagine that in your class, there are three or four lads who want to read Shakespeare or Goethe. Imagine that other students have no wish to read these authors. So what will you do if you are a 'democratic' teacher? You will let your students decide what they wish to study. No Shakespeare, no Goethe, to be sure. A couple of modern mediocre authors instead. The result is that your students will become low-minded or just narrow-minded persons — selfish and loathsome, in fact. But your work will surely be admired and applauded by all 'friends of Democracy.'

Or imagine for a moment that you have become a priest. So what will you preach to your parish? Will you advise people to get rid of their hatred and ignorance? Well, just try to annoy them by sermons of this kind. There surely will be another preacher just around the corner, someone who tells them that Jesus loves all of them. Without excepting murderers, harlots, and liars. (You know, any true bodhisattva[41] loves harlots and liars, but not precisely because they *are* harlots and liars.) He will tell that Jesus Himself is a great friend of Democracy. It is his church, not yours, that will get crowded, it's he who will get his money, and it's he who will win. And it's you who will lose. It's you who

---

[40] 'Too bad' — *L. R.*

[41] In Mahayana Buddhism, a bodhisattva refers to anyone who has generated bodhicitta, a spontaneous wish and compassionate mind to attain Buddhahood for the benefit of all sentient beings — *L. R.*

will be cynically asked, 'If you're so smart, why are you so poor?'

Meanwhile, think, how could Jesus be a friend of Democracy? A 'democrat' wishes to make people equal. Jesus, who never was equal to other people, wanted His followers to be like Him. I think He wanted them to *differ* from each other, to go their own way. The Buddha, too, valued variety among His disciples, and we know it for certain.

You will ask me what you are to do in this brave new world and which way you are to go.

Stop wishing to be mediocre. Dare to be cleverer than others. Look up for the splits of the old aristocratic culture. Study them carefully. You may find genuine gems among those splits as I have found them in European music. Forget about your democratic rights. Realise that you are very far from being a Buddha.[42] Realise that at the moment you look much more like a swine than a human being. Then search for a good tyrant for your mind, a true Kshatriya who would be honest, clever, and strong. Search for someone who will bind you and beat you until your hatred, lust, and ignorance are dead forever.[43] You will be happy if you find a good tyrant. But there are only few of them left in the age of Democracy. So become your own slave and your own tyrant in case you cannot find one. The freedom of the modern world leads to slavery, but your freewill slavery will lead you to the Ultimate Freedom. Go to war. Go to the war with your *obscurations*.[44] Never forget that your obscurations are strong. That they may kill you before you kill them. Then fight. Struggle with all your might. Never listen to the shouts of the crowd. People

---

[42] According to the Tibetan Buddhism, everyone has the potential to attain Buddhahood — *L. R.*

[43] Hopefully, the reader understands that it is said metaphorically — *L. R.*

[44] An obscuration (Sanskrit: *klesha*) is a negative mental state that clouds the mind and manifests in unwholesome actions. *Kleshas* include states of mind such as anxiety, fear, anger, jealousy, desire, depression, etc. — *L. R.*

of the crowd seem to be much cleverer than you, but it will be you, not them, whom your obscurations will murder if you keep listening to the crowd. Never stop this most noble fight. You will win sooner or later. This is something the Tathagata[45] promised to all His soldiers. Don't you believe Him, the Tathagata? Then what do you believe in? In Democracy? A miserable belief. Don't care about friends of Democracy. Why should you care about them? Why should you be afraid of them? There is only one thing that is worth caring about. The total enlightenment of all living beings. There is only one thing that is worth being afraid of. The vice. So be an aristocrat if the Buddha used to be one. Be a prince. Be the monarch of your own mind.

---

[45] The Buddha, literally 'The One Thus Gone' — L. R.

Worlds

A demon, an angel, and a human being are looking at a glass filled with something wet and flowing. The demon sees it as pus and blood, the man as water, the angel as ambrosia.

In reality, the content of the glass has the nature of water, blood, and ambrosia at the same time. Our perception is capable of perceiving only the reality corresponding to our mind.

Some modern machines allow us to understand how it happens. Imagine a broad plate of metal with many small balls of the same metal on it. There are some spots where the plate gets warm from outer sources. We take an infra-red photo of it in the dark. This photo will hardly give us any opportunity to see the small balls. It is only hot spots we will see on the photo. The metal has at the same time two true natures: that of form and that of temperature. A normal camera is able to grasp only the first one, whereas an infra-red camera is capable of 'seeing' only that of temperature, as long as there is no light in the room.

We are able to perceive only something we *are* or we have within ourselves. In case you are a physician you notice diseases of others. In case you are a master of rhetoric or, say, a phonetician you notice the way one speaks. If you are a lama you notice obscurations and mental poisons of a person. Each of us has, in fact, the three natures I have just named: those of body, speech, and mind. We can notice all the three at the same time only if we are attentive enough.

I don't think I am saying something you didn't know before. Everything I have just said is well-known to everyone who studies Abhidharma. The problem of glass filled with something wet and flowing is well-known in our scriptures. It is called 'analysis of water' or *chu bab*.[46] Many Western students of Buddhism regard this problem as something purely theoretic, scholastic, being out of touch with real life. One seldom sees a demon or an angel in one's everyday life, to say the truth.

Your belief in *chu bab* being out of touch with real life is not our problem. It is yours. You are convinced that each scriptural question is out of touch with it. I am unable to draw a line between Christianity and pseudo-Christianity, as there is Buddhism and pseudo-Buddhism. And yet, I think that many pseudo-Christian beliefs are built upon lies. Upon the false idea that an eternal romantic love does exist, for instance. On the belief that each religious person is capable of becoming prosperous. That almost all so-called Christians are followers of Jesus. And so on. If one doesn't find in one's everyday reality manifestations of ideas one was taught, the person begins to believe that these ideas are false. Yet in case one is religious enough, one still believes them to exist somewhere in another world. Beyond this life. You grew used to this idea. We Asians didn't.

The analysis of water is very pragmatic.

The liquid has at least three true natures. Why not four or ten, then? Doesn't it mean that each thing has a numerous variety of natures? It really has, believe me.

The Universe is made of things. To be more exact, the world consists of things. Worlds consist of them. You are naïve if you think that only one world exists[47] and that this only world is inhabited by demons, human beings, semi-gods, and gods at the same

---

[46] The problem of *chu bab* is handled at length in the *Overview of the Middle Way*, composed by Khedrup Tenpa Dargye, a Tibetan scholar (1493 — 1568), who, in his turn, analyses *Entering the Middle Way*, or *Madhyamakaavatara*, by Chandrakirti (~650 AD) — *L. R.*

[47] At the first glance, this statement seems to contradict to what Rinpoche says before in 'Consumers'. A few lines further on, we clearly see that there is no contradiction — *L. R.*

time. Old Indian and Tibetan myths tell about gods living in the sky. Some centuries ago one still could believe it. Now airplanes and spaceships go across the sky, and no pilot, no astronaut has ever seen any angel. We certainly would see them if they lived in our world, wouldn't we? It proves that many worlds exist.

I don't mean they exist ultimately. *There is only one world.* At the same time, there are many of them. The only world is inhabited by very different beings. What sense does it make to speak about this one world, though, if we human beings never perceive its other inhabitants? Most of us are surely not capable of perceiving them. In the ultimate sense, no different worlds exist. Neither do buddhas, yidams, samsara and Nirvana exist, nor is there any suffering, nor the Path. This is what *Prajña Paramita Hridaya Sutra*[48] states. Who needs this very subtle wisdom, then? This wisdom is similar to silk. Silk is a very good material for pajamas, yet you won't use it for warm winter clothes. You are hardly able to use silk in your everyday life.

Many worlds do exist. They are created by minds of sentient beings. 'Created' is a wrong word, though. I would rather say, 'separated.' In the beginning, someone appears who is not capable of perceiving the whole world as it is, whose perception now sets something this being *can* perceive apart from the rest of the world, so that one can inhabit this part. Then someone with similar perception appears. Thus grows the population of the isolated part of the world which part now becomes a separate world. Transition from one world to another is possible. It is possible without any wings, simply by altering our perception. You probably know about the Buddha's ability to preach simultaneously to both human beings and *nagas*[49]. How could He do it at

---

[48] Or the *Heart Sutra*, probably the most popular scripture of Mahayana Buddhism — L. R.

[49] The *naga* in Buddhism are divine, semi-divine deities, or a semi-divine race of half-human half-serpent beings that reside in the netherworld (Patala) and can occasionally take human form — L. R.

the same time in case nagas really lived somewhere in the underground kingdom as our old myths say?

Our human perception is more or less the same. You know, such names as 'demon,' 'angel,' or 'human being' are quite conventional. Demons and angels differ from us neither because of their thin necks[50] nor because of their radiant skin. They differ from us because of their different perception. Perception is primary. Substance of our bodies is secondary. No sooner than our perception alters do we become able to alter energies that vitalise our body. These energies are similar to electricity. Our body is similar to a lamp. As soon as there is no electricity the light of the lamp dies out. A man simply dies. Having altered our perception, we gradually can replace one kind of electricity by another one. The very substance of our body alters after this substitution. The realisation of the *vajra* body[51] by some lamas is exactly what I mean. I also think that Jesus, too, was capable of altering the substance of His body. He did it, for instance, immediately after His resurrection.[52] I don't think He could stay alive in another case, after getting heavy wounds one cannot live with.

From this point of view I can understand why you call Him a god.[53] Someone capable of seeing gods and talking to them can surely be called one. Will you call your cat a human being in case he or she talks to you? I doubt of it. However, if your cat puts on trousers and a shirt, goes to an office, and earns some money,

---

[50] A characteristic feature of the *preta*, a class of Buddhist demons — L. R.

[51] The *vajra* body is a body 'made of bliss and emptiness', the state of a pure and immaterial body into which the ordinary body may be transformed by spiritual efforts. Rinpoche refers to some very rare cases of lamas whose physical remnants had never been discovered after their death — L. R.

[52] The idea of Jesus Christ 'having realised a vajra body' certainly disagrees with Christian beliefs according to which Jesus was raised from the dead by God, not by His own spiritual efforts. It is remarkable, though, that Rinpoche tries to conceptualise Christianity in Buddhist terms, however naïve such attempts may sound for a Christian — L. R.

[53] Again most Christians would disagree as the difference between 'a god' and 'the God' is obvious for any Christian — L. R.

you doubtlessly will regard your cat as a human being. This point of view allows us to call the Buddha a god, too, because the Buddha had many conversations with gods. He also may be called a naga, because He preached to them. You see, these names are merely conventional. As well as the word 'man.' Using the same word 'man' for a saint man and a murderer seems quite strange to me. Yes, my astonishment doesn't easily comply with your 'democratic' beliefs, with your conviction that people are equal to each other. However, if you deal with this idea using the method of *prasanga*[54] it becomes simply ridiculous. In case people have equal rights, animals should get the same rights, shouldn't they? Who told you that people are more cultivated than animals? What makes you think that? What are you guided by in saying people are better than animals? By animal fur? Judging only by their fur, you discriminate animals in the same way you discriminated blacks by the colour of their skin. Are you racists, then? Do you judge by the fact that animals cannot speak?[55] Do you regard mentally disabled persons as animals, then? Or is it the size of a being that decides? Doesn't it sound like humiliation of midgets, then? And so on it goes.

The conventional word 'people' signifies a huge number of very different beings. These beings are so different, that some of them live in different worlds, in the way demons and angels do, and never get in touch with each other.

First of all, I mean social worlds.

You probably will tell me that I am mistaken. You tell me that it is true for Asia, not for Europe, where democracy rules. You believe you have no boundaries between social classes, or strata.

---

[54] *Prasanga* a method of *reductio ad absurdum* which is used by Buddhist scholars, using syllogisms to point out the absurd and impossible logical consequences of holding opponents' views — L. R.

[55] The example of Koko the Gorilla and other such examples probably show that animals *can* speak — L. R.

You are partly right. In Europe, even a poor person can enter a shop for the rich (one can attempt it, at least), and even a rich person may have a mistress from a ghetto. However, your social worlds are as well separated from each other as ours. You may tell me that I am wrong when I use this metaphor speaking of social classes. After all, the poor can see the rich, unlike angels or demons. You know, it is you who is mistaken. A rich person doesn't perceive any poor one. He or she sees only an insect[56] in its place. Be honest. You people of the West succeeded in creating numerous fairytales about Cinderella marrying a prince. About a millionaire marrying a prostitute.[57] Do you really believe in your fairytales? In reality, a poor person, too, regards the rich as insects. Huge and dangerous insects, but their size matters nothing. It is exactly so, believe me.

Each social class, each stratum regards itself as the most important one, as the only 'real' one, and sees people of other classes as outsiders, losers. And maybe even as scoundrels. The rich despise prostitutes as much as prostitutes despise the rich. In the same way you condescendingly ignore people of Asia, people of Asia condescendingly ignore you.[58] A poor man surely can enter a shop for the rich, but he or she doesn't want it. Most poor people despise consumption and men with a thick wallet; to them, the joys of the rich are contemptible. They probably will change their opinion in case they suddenly grow rich, you know. A prostitute is not prohibited to go to a library, to a bookstore, or to a concert hall. But she never goes to any of these places. She thinks of books as rubbish; she believes that intellectuals are worthless and weak creatures. Her life would be unbearable if she didn't think so. Wealthy Indians or Arabs sometimes visit Europe. Does it matter anything? While staying in Europe, they

---

[56] I hesitated for a while whether to keep the word or to replace it by 'nonentity' etc. It looks like it is not easily replaceable — L. R.

[57] I think Rinpoche refers to *Pretty Woman*, a 1990 American romantic comedy film — L. R.

[58] A very gloomy picture. What if it is true to some extent? — L. R.

listen to the Arabic music, watch Arabic TV shows, and eat Arabic dishes. Their business partners, too, speak Arabic. So they stay within their own Arabic world, just because the European music, European dishes and, first of all, European values are not very attractive[59] to them. That is why your worlds never get in touch. Two business partners, a European and an Indian, shake hands and smile to each other.

However, there is no Indian in the mental space of the European. No unique Hindu-individual exists there. The European only sees a lazy and ignorant citizen of the third world, full of complexes and religious prejudices. In the same way no European, as he sees himself, exists in the world of the Indian. There is only a shameless and ignorant person there, a person with no religion and no true values, a person no-one takes seriously. Of course I exaggerate a bit.[60] The best of my students are neither shameless nor ignorant. The people here don't regard us Tibetans as a primitive nation, I suppose. Some Western people are able to see good sides of other nations; they can appreciate them and even admire them. You believe that every one of you is capable of it. In fact, such persons are few in number.

Transitions from one world to another are possible, as I have just mentioned. In most cases, however, these transitions are not like the Buddha's, who was aware of His human experience while communicating with gods and of His heavenly experience while communicating with men. People just 'emigrate'. Someone suddenly inherits a large sum of money and 'emigrates' to the world of the rich. Now he or she stops despising consumption. He or she rather begins to despise his or her former comrades. It is a bit more difficult than just hypocrisy. Everyone has one's own advantages and shortcomings. The inhabitants of one world are able to clearly see all shortcomings of other worlds. Their own

---

[59] The first edition had 'loathsome' — *L. R.*
[60] A relief to hear that — *L. R.*

ones remain hidden from them. Someone who instantly became rich easily sees vices of the poor. Someone who suddenly became poor easily sees sins of the rich. A Buddhist clearly perceives defects of Christianity. A Christian clearly perceives defects of Buddhism.[61]

There are two more reasons for isolation of different social worlds.

The first one is modern communication technologies: the Internet and the social media. Some decades ago, a musician went to visit another musician along a real street in a real town, and he met different persons on his way: a butcher, say, or this-funny-old-lady-who-lives-round-the-corner. Now you can contact anyone over the web, without seeing other persons. Each social group can now separate itself from the society and keep out of touch with other groups.

The second and more important one is the Western idea of tolerance.

Tolerance comes from 'to tolerate,' I suppose. Tolerance means tolerating others. We let others be. Tolerance is not the same with love. It also has nothing in common with hatred. Tolerance is simply indifference. Nothing separates people more than indifference.

You see, there are three roots of evil: lust, hatred, and ignorance. And the last one is actually very close to indifference. Lust comes from our selfish desires; hatred comes from anger. Indifference comes from ignorance. If you ask me, which root of evil is the worst one, I will answer, 'It is indifference.'

---

[61] Speaking of the 'defects' of both sorts Rinpoche probably means the natural uneasiness one feels when encountering a completely different system of beliefs — L. R.

Even hatred keeps different worlds in touch. The West was not always tolerant. You people of the West used to burn your magicians and witches alive. You had your great religious wars. The middle ages of Europe certainly were awful. However, your religious wars couldn't proceed at a distance. One always gets in touch with one's own enemy. You have to cognise your enemy, to study him thoroughly if you want to defeat him. While studying our enemy, we learn his good sides as well. We begin to respect him. There is no definite border between the domain of *devas*[62] and the *asura*[63] sphere, as you can see it on the *bhavacakra*.[64] Why so? Because devas are continually fighting with asuras. Even the Buddha learnt a big deal about demonic nature while fighting with Mara.[65] One of the *jatakas*[66] states that the Buddha, too, in one of His former lives was Yama, the king of hell. Tell it no one, please. Things like this one are not for European ears. Two thirds of Europeans would immediately accuse us of being Satanists as soon as they learnt about the Buddha being the king of hell.[67]

You may tell that tolerance, too, requires respect for your partner. It may require it in some treatise on tolerance. Of what use is this requirement, though, if in reality there is no respect at all? Respect never arises without prior understanding of a person. Understanding never arises without compassion.

You believe tolerance to be a feature of Buddhism. Some of you even believe that the Buddha preached tolerance. Nothing of the

---

[62] Gods of popular Tibetan mythology — *L. R.*

[63] Semi-gods of popular Tibetan mythology — *L. R.*

[64] The bhavacakra, or 'the Wheel of Life', is a symbolic representation of the 'human universe' — *L. R.*

[65] Mara in Buddhism is the powerful demon who tempted the Buddha. Resisting Mara's temptations is sometimes, even if seldom, metaphorically described as 'fighting with Mara' — *L. R.*

[66] The *Jataka* tales are a voluminous body of literature concerning the previous births of the Buddha in both human and animal form — *L. R.*

[67] Rinpoche probably means to say that myths and legends must be interpreted metaphorically — *L. R.*

kind. It was compassion He preached. I will never believe that the Buddha accepted a courtesan's invitation to a dinner out of simple tolerance.[68] Visiting a hetaera by a buddha goes beyond tolerance. For a person we just tolerate, two polite phrases and a hypocritical smile are enough. It was compassion that moved the Buddha to finally accept the invitation of Ambapali. It was compassion that moved Him to establish the order of nuns.[69] It was compassion that forced Him to leave His family, for He wanted to discover a medicine for each and any suffering. It was compassion, not tolerance, He was motivated by for the length of His life.

Neither did your teacher, Jesus, preach tolerance. Jesus was not tolerant. Not at the moment He expelled merchants from the temple. This deed probably led Him to His crucifixion, for similar causes produce similar results. Even bodhisattvas obey the law of karma.[70] I am not going to say that this deed was a bad or a wrong one. You have to defend the right cause even at risk of being hurt. Anyway, Jesus was ready to face the consequences. You His disciples believe that the law of karma comes from God, that it is ultimately fair and good. Why should it be? It was karma that killed Jesus and hurt the Buddha's foot,[71] wasn't it? Was it fair, then? Was it good? Who profited from the Buddha's

---

[68] In ancient India, there was a custom to invite monks and ascetics to a meal during which ceremony rich donations could also be made. (This tradition has survived in some Buddhist countries until now.) Ambapali, a celebrated royal courtesan, invited the Buddha and His order to a meal, and He accepted the invitation — L. R.

[69] According to the Pali canon, the Buddha was very unwilling to establish the order of nuns and only did it out of compassion for His aunt, a holy woman, who had a strong urge to become a nun — L. R.

[70] This very Buddhist view on Christ who, like every other being, had to obey the law of karma is in all probability unacceptable for any Christian. And yet, I cannot help recalling *Pilatus* ('Pilate'), a 1967 novel by Alexander Lernet-Holenia (1897–1976), an Austrian poet and novelist. It is now impossible to find out if Rinpoche was familiar with this novel and its paradoxical conclusions
— L. R.

[71] Devadatta, a malicious disciple, injured the Buddha's foot by a big stone
— L. R.

wound but Mara? There is no more justice in the law of karma than in a bulldozer.

Tolerance is an unnatural, a perverted idea. A man is never indifferent to his enemies or friends. We cannot help loving Good. We cannot help detesting Evil. As *Lamrimchenmo* of the glorious Je Tsongkhapa[72] states, this hatred is the only hatred that is beneficial to us. We must detest Evil. We must fight with it. We must do it without detesting the person poisoned by Evil. Or should we just tolerate Evil, in accordance with the modern 'democratic' values? Should we just let it be? Let it be, then, if it corresponds to your idea of democracy. But you won't achieve Liberation this way. Unfortunately for some of you, the Buddha's Path is not a democratic one. Why not accuse the Buddha and Jesus of assault to human rights? In some decades you most likely will do just that.

Tolerance produces indifference. It separates worlds. 'Let them be as they are,' this is how an indifferent person thinks. 'I don't care.' It is not only worlds of different social classes and not only those of different religions that exist, though.

We live not only among things.[73] It is ideas we live among. There still are some people who read ancient poets. These people live in the world of Ancient Greece or Ancient Rome. There still are persons who admire your beautiful music of the nineteenth century. They live in their separate world, too. Neither did the twentieth, nor the nineteenth, nor the eighteenth century with their corresponding worlds ever cease to be. These worlds and the modern world exist at the same time. The same planet is inhabited by both murderers and saints, by both merchants and monks, by both computer programmers and inquisitors. By both angels and demons. By both those who are in hell and those who

---

[72] Je Tsongkhapa (1357 — 1419), a famous teacher of Tibetan Buddhism — L. R.

[73] 'We live among things' is a very Heideggerian idea — L. R.

are in Heaven. The same country, the same city, or even the same house can be one's Heaven and another's hell. It is our perception that decides where we are.

I shall tell a few words about Heaven and hell, or, more exactly, the Heaven and the hell, about two things you don't believe in. Your mind cannot simply cease to be after your death. Neither changes the world we live in. In is your perception that changes. A dog doesn't perceive colours.[74] A person whose mind is poisoned by the vice cannot help seeing Evil in the outer world. In reality, the Heaven and the hell can exist at the same place and at the same time. If one's house can be one's hell before his death, why cannot hell exist *after* one's death? You are mistaken if you think that popular descriptions of hell are just myths and legends. The liquid we human beings call 'water' simultaneously has the nature of water, blood, and ambrosia. The air we breathe has at the same time the nature both of endless heat and of infinite cold that can bring insufferable pain. Do you notice that you feel cold when you are ashamed? The air temperature doesn't change at the moments you feel cold out of shame. Quite the same happens after your death, when you feel cold or hot out of the same shame. These sensations are much more intense, though. The shell of your body protects you while you are alive. The body is coarse, and those coarse sensations drown more subtle impulses. After your death, there is no more protection provided by your body, and your mind becomes defenseless.

However, all these beings we conventionally call 'men' or 'women' don't care two pence for other worlds — the worlds one enters much easier than the pure land of the Buddha Amitabha![75] Going to a library, or to a monastery, or to a Buddhist institute actually *takes* you to a new world.

------

[74] Behavioral tests suggest that dogs see in shades of yellow and blue and lack the ability to see the range of colours from green to red — L. R.

[75] 'The Pure Land of the Buddha Amitabha' is another name for *Sukhavati*, or 'the Western Paradise', in Tibetan Buddhism — L. R.

You see, there is the selfishness of suffering as well as there is the selfishness of happiness. Someone who suffers despises happy men and never cares for them. Someone who is happy seldom cares for those who suffer. There also is a completely false concept of Liberation as transition to another world. There is no Liberation in one of the local worlds, nor can there be any, just because the perception of worlds' inhabitants is limited. If it were *not* limited, they could see other worlds along with their inhabitants, they could, in fact, see the whole Universe. A limited being cannot be ultimately happy, so it cannot be free. Life in each of the worlds is *samsara*[76]. Transition from one limited world to another is samsara either.

The Buddha didn't limit Himself by the social world of the Sangha, the brotherhood He created by Himself. Once you asked me whether a single being can create a world. Here you have an answer. It was the Buddha who created the whole world of the Buddhist monkshood. This world is still inhabited by crowds of people. This world has regular countries, such as Thailand or Sri Lanka where the Sangha is the very centre of social life. The Buddha created a world. Yet He didn't stay within it. He was in touch with kings and servants, with saint men and murderers. Remember Angulimala[77]. With the Hindus and pagans. With ascetics and hetaeras. Remember Ambapali. He was interested in each one. Why then? Because He didn't divide our world into sections. He didn't think one profession, nation, or religion to be better than another one. He did not do what most people do. He saw our world as an entity. He didn't limit His perception by one idea. He didn't see people only from the viewpoint of a lama, or that of a monk, or that of a preacher. Long ago, a

---

[76] *Samsara* is a Sanskrit word that means 'wandering' or 'world,' with the connotation of cyclic, circuitous change. In short, it is the cycle of death and rebirth, the cycle of aimless drifting, wandering or mundane existence. Samsara is opposed to Nirvana, or a blissful state beyond any suffering — L. R.

[77] Angulimala, a half-legendary figure, was as a ruthless brigand who completely transformed after his conversion to Buddhism. His story can be found in numerous sources in Pali, Sanskrit, Tibetan and Chinese. — L. R.

Buddhist monk saw a woman and was proud of his inability to determine the sex of the person he saw. The monk saw only a skeleton. This monk never guessed that the Buddha saw other people in quite a different way. The Buddha didn't see only skeletons around Him. You see, it is difficult to feel compassion for a skeleton. There can be no doubt that the Buddha felt compassion for anyone.

And thus He perceived the whole world. This is why everyone listened to Him. Men and animals, demons and bodhisattvas, nagas and gods gave attention to His words. This is why He simultaneously was in every world. This is why He was a man, a god, and a demon at the same time. Yes, even a demon He had been, long before His last incarnation when he became a buddha. He wouldn't be able to defeat demons if He never had been one of them, at least for an instant. This is why He saw the world as a whole, not cut into different worlds in the same way you cut ham into slices. This very entity of the only world is called Liberation or Nirvana.

Nirvana is the highest goal we can have before our eyes. One cannot achieve Nirvana without following the Buddha, with out going along His path.[78] His path is regarding the world as an entity.

Begin with human worlds. Just stop thinking of your profession as being the best one. Realise that there are many professions more difficult and more important than yours. A Christian should give up his belief in Christianity being an exclusive path to Heaven; he or she should look into the Buddhist world to see

---

[78] This may be read as (over)emphasising the exceptional role of Buddhism which for some Buddhists reassuringly proves that Rinpoche was a very orthodox teacher and which is of course unacceptable for the Christian readership. However, in his sermon entitled 'Four Truths' (it is the last chapter of this book) Rinpoche distinctly speaks of Christianity as of an alternative path to 'Liberation' — L. R.

his or her own bad sides from another viewpoint. A Buddhist should do the same with the world of Christianity. People of the West should reject the idea of their being the best people on earth; they should look at the way they live from the Asian viewpoint. We people of Asia should do the same with us, when thinking of the West. Everyone could occasionally read authors one has never read before, listen to the music one has never heard before, to realise why others enjoy it. Everyone should give up the useless concept of tolerance in order to embrace the idea of understanding other people and sincere compassion for them. Will it suffice for Liberation? Certainly not. But it will be of much importance for us. We probably won't achieve enlightenment immediately after listening to a symphony of Beethoven or reading the Prajña Paramita Hridaya Sutra. However, if we believe that neither Beethoven nor the Hridaya Sutra is of any use for reaching Liberation, we will never achieve it. The world is one. It is only our perception that divides it into samsara and Nirvana, into the poor and the rich, into the West and the East, into Christianity and Buddhism, into Heaven and hell. Dividing the one world enslaves the divider.

Women

I often hear women say, 'We must be independent from men. We can do everything. We don't need men at all. We are going to rule over the world.' And so on.

Sayings like these are partly justified, partly not. Yet everyone who takes them too literally also thinks that once, some centuries or decades ago, the real men, courageous and strong, did exist, and then, all of a sudden, they died out, so that women are to go without them now.

This image is quite naïve. First of all, you should consider the fact that men and women are not yet so different as fish and birds, as horses and sheep. The same mind incarnates into either a male or female human body. Someone who once had been a man can be reborn as a woman, and vice versa. You probably say that it happens seldom, that, once used to a male body, the person keeps being reborn as a male. Let us temporarily assume you are right. Human minds continuously incarnate into new bodies. It means — provided you are right about men staying men — that those persons who now are in male bodies had been also incarnated as men many centuries ago, in the middle ages, let us say. At that time, men were courageous and strong. So why should *the same minds* suddenly degenerate?

They never did, in fact. The truth is that living as a man is more difficult. It only applies to the period we live in, and to the West.

Your Western culture of today is a culture of consumption. To be more exact, a culture of lust. Lust is only one of the leading forces that determine human existence. Cultures of anger or cultures of reason exist as well. Most of Eastern cultures are those of reason that balances anger and lust. The Western culture was always inclined to follow one of the two extremes.

Any culture of anger allows and justifies anger, but bans pleasures. It sees any pleasure as Evil. Your European culture of the middle ages was that of anger. Your inquisitors had burnt at the stake a lot of women because of their female longing for pleasure.[79]

Any culture of lust deals with pleasure in the opposite way. It prohibits anger and it calls any anger shameful while allowing pleasure. You see: it is exactly the morality you Westerners share now. At present, you can be arrested and imprisoned in case you kill even an animal. But you may have as many sexual partners as you wish. Nobody will mind it. The situation was quite different five centuries ago. At that time, nobody would mind your killing two or three persons, especially in case you could prove that the killed ones had been magicians, witches, or pagans. But if you attempted to have many partners you probably would be burnt alive.

Anger is degraded fire[80] which in its pure form exists as will. Lust is corrupted water which in its pure form exists as compassion. Fire is male. Water is female.

In a fire culture, women hardly can be successful. In a water culture (which your culture now is), being a man is a hard task. No man can ever be as successful as women when dealing with pleasure. A man thinks and feels differently. However, the society limits his pride, forbids his anger, and forces him to be sensual. Without sensuality, he can succeed neither in the spiritual domain nor in the social life. In case he is a writer, he has to create texts inspired by desire. In case his profession requires

---

[79] I probably must note that Pope John Paul II made an apology for the Church's role in burnings at the stake in May 1995 in the Czech Republic, and for the injustices committed against women on May 29, 1995, in a 'letter to women' — L. R.

[80] Rinpoche refers to traditional terms of the Tibetan medicine: *fire* (or bile) and *water* (or phlegm) — L. R.

communication with customers, he must do it in the way that would please them. Even in case he is a simple manual worker, his muscular power is required much less than his ability to listen to the wishes of his customer — or his boss, maybe. Any man does this worse than almost any woman. As a result, some men accept this quite humiliating[81] situation and become womanlike. Women dislike such men. This is how lesbian love appears. Other men neglect the necessity of being 'pleasant' and give up their social prospects at all. These men are regarded by women as losers. So what kind of men does a modern woman see around herself? Either womanlike creatures or losers. Therefore, she believes that 'the real men' have ceased to be. Only a very small number of men are capable of finding an occupation that would still require their anger and will. They become soldiers or policemen. These professions are rare in the culture of lust, and this is why men who wear a uniform are still wanted by women. The general mood changed from one extreme to the other. The women of the West were enslaved for a millennium of years, now they triumph over their former enslavers.

I feel very sorry for Western men, but I don't know what I shall advise them. They probably should stay manlike, however much the culture of lust might provoke them to be the opposite. They ought to limit their pleasures; to give up the idea of consumption; to cultivate courage more than pity or, more exactly, sentimentality you falsely regard as compassion. It is difficult, though. Going against the mainstream is always difficult.

The subject of this discourse is women, not men, so let us talk about women. I don't think the women who are sitting here came here to look up for pleasures. I believe many of you are faithful Buddhist women. At least, you pretend to be them. But what *is* a Buddhist woman? What is she to do? Buddhism is, to

---

[81] It is of course arguable whether the need to meet customers' expectations is 'humiliating' or not, but I must admit that this very straightforward description strikes a chord with me — L. R.

be honest, a man-like religion. For many centuries and even millennia it was supported by men. Buddhism is convenient to men. What about women? Becoming manlike, being like men (an inferior kind), is not the best solution.

However, the images of successful Buddhist women exist. They have existed for ages. They already existed at the time of the Buddha.

There are at least four women the Tathagata appreciated. I am going to name them one after another, from the least to the most important one.

Ambapali, a courtesan.

Mahaprajapati Gautami, the Buddha's aunt.

Yashodhara, the Buddha's wife.

Mahamaya, the Buddha's mother.

Let us begin with the courtesan. A *hetaera* is not the same as a prostitute. We call a prostitute a woman who has sexual intercourse with anyone who pays her, no matter whether she likes her client or not. A hetaera is much more someone you call a mistress. A courtesan has one or many lovers she chooses by herself. She gets money from them, but in return she gives them her genuine love. It is love, not only sexual pleasure, she gives to her lovers. You see, love is much more valuable than just physical relations. I think courtesans used to be very rich. So rich that Ambapali was able to invite the whole Sangha of the Buddha for a meal. Many hundreds of monks were invited. As a rule, only kings did it.

I want to emphasise that the Buddha accepted the invitation. He probably was the most holy man who ever lived.[82] He would never accept an invitation of a person whom He considered to be vile. Why, getting in touch with a vile person could do much harm to the Sangha. The Buddha was full of compassion, but *tolerant* in the sense in which you use the word He definitely wasn't. It seems to be that He didn't regard Ambapali, the courtesan, as a vile person.

If we start reflecting what courtesan life was like we suddenly realise that courtesans lived exactly in the way in which most of modern women of the West do. Consider that hetaeras found their lovers by themselves. They sometimes had many lovers at the same time, which situation a modern woman believes to be all right. As soon as they wanted to leave their lovers they did it. They were independent and had their own money. They communicated with anyone they wanted to get in touch with, be it a murderer or a saint. You see, Buddhism accepts the way in which modern Western women live. However, we Buddhists don't think it to be the best way of life. No-one of us puts Ambapali on the same level as the Buddha's mother, wife, or aunt. We just accept it. One remark should be added: we accept 'independent women', but we only respect them in case they sometimes do important and unselfish deeds. If they invite the Sangha for a meal, for instance. Or if they donate a considerable sum to a hospital. This is how a faithful woman should act.

A better example of a Buddhist woman is Mahaprajapati Gautami[83], the Buddha's aunt, the first Buddhist nun. As you know, it took her much time to persuade the Buddha that a female Sangha has the right to be. The Buddha surely was right when He doubted of it. Women shouldn't simply copy men's behaviour. However, the Buddha allowed Mahaprajapati to enter the

---

[82] Again a very dubitable statement for every Christian — *L. R.*
[83] The Pali spelling of her name is Mahapajapati Gotami — *L. R.*

Sangha. The Buddha did nothing without good reasons. It means that becoming a nun is as well a way of life for a Buddhist woman, probably not the worst one.

The Buddha created for female members of His Sangha eight important rules[84] each nun is to keep in addition to the common monastic vows. Those rules gave to some Buddhists an opportunity to say that a Buddhist nun, when compared with a Buddhist monk, should make stronger efforts to achieve Liberation. You probably ask me whether it is so. Surely it is. Not because each woman is a vile creature, inferior to men, and not because of menses, and not because of other imaginary matters your European mind creates. The culture of monkshood is that of will. Both renunciation and keeping vows require much will. Monks' culture is that of anger, to some extent. You see, a monk must detest his obscurations. He must detest them, not tolerate them. The concept of tolerance is absolutely false for a monk. Within a culture of anger, a woman is always less successful than a man, as well as a man is always less successful than a woman within a culture of pleasure. It was compassion, not contempt, out of which the Buddha didn't want to allow women to enter the Buddhist nunhood. He didn't want those women to go the way of modern men who have to give up essential features of their sex for the sake of their success.

However, there are some men who earn their living as designers. So why cannot there be some women who observe monastic vows? Some nuns on their path to Liberation achieved spiritual results most men are only dreaming of. Should we despise their achievements just because of their sex? In their case, the end justifies the means.

---

[84] The 'Eight Heavy Dharmas', or *ashta garu dharma*, are first mentioned in the Pali canon — L. R.

The Buddha surely knew that nunhood is not very suitable for women. You probably ask me, why the Buddha didn't create another community, based on other rules. The answer is easy: the Buddha Himself was a man. He could not run a female organisation just because of that. If He did, some slanderers certainly would accuse Him of providing Himself with an opportunity for sexual enjoyments. Slanderous accusations of the Buddha were numerous even without that. Never believe any slanderer. To run a female organisation, the Buddha had to incarnate into a female body. However, if He were a woman He would never gain authority necessary for spreading His Dharma. He would not even be able to learn from Arada Kalama and Udraka Ramaputra, His teachers. Why, those teachers were men and ran male communities no woman could enter.

Another more beautiful example of a Buddhist woman is the Buddha's wife, the princess Yashodhara[85]. She is a typical woman, so to say. She was her husband's wife, not a hetaera; she always complied with Indian traditions. Yashodhara was a good mother and an excellent wife; otherwise, the Buddha would not praise her so much. What was it that made her an excellent wife, though? Believing in her husband. Following Him. Unfortunately, she could not follow her husband literally.[86] And yet, the canon states that she shaved her head as soon as she learnt that her husband did it. As soon as she heard about her husband keeping the fast she started fasting, too. And so on. I do believe that her father-in-law, the king Shuddhodana[87], quite disliked her religious practices. I think everyone was against them. No-one supported her. Even religion couldn't give her any support. Today, we are happy to know that her husband became a buddha. Yashodhara couldn't possibly know it. She only heard different and contradictory opinions on Him. Someone said her

---

[85] Another spelling of her name is Yasodhara — L. R.

[86] Yashodhara couldn't follow her husband in his radical asceticism since no asceticism for women was (easily) possible at that time. – L. R.

[87] Another spelling of his name is Suddhodana — L. R.

husband had become a saint, other people believed her former husband was nuts.[88] Be it as it may, she never gave up her faith in Him. She imitated Him. This is why each Buddhist woman may well imitate her. You probably say that you see no difference between the Buddhist ideal of a wife and that of Hinduism. You are mistaken. There *is* a difference between them. A Hindu woman loves without reflecting on her love. On the day of her marriage, she is given to her husband without being asked for her consent. This may or may not result in a happy marriage, but it is not something you Western women would enjoy. Yashodhara, unlike Hindu women, could choose her husband by herself. Many men wanted to marry her. The pretenders even competed in a sportive contest. She had her free choice. And she chose one who became a buddha. Pay attention to the fact that she never regretted her choice. This is how a Buddhist woman should act. She has to choose her future husband thoroughly. She is to find one to whom being married she will never regret. Well, she also can become a hetaera or a nun. These ways of life are open to her as well. However, the Buddhist canon mentions the Buddha's wife much more often than Ambapali, the courtesan. No wonder.

Ambapali, Prajapati, and Yashodhara are good women. However, there is another one we Buddhists esteem even more than the Buddha's wife. It is His mother.

Maya[89] the queen was a good wife. And even more than that she was. Maya was a heroine. Once in her dream she saw a white elephant, and the elephant revealed to her that she would give birth to an outstanding person. This is what a Buddhist legend says. I don't think this legend to be false. Each legend simplifies reality, though. Maya the queen most likely had many conversations with the white elephant and with different deities over

---

[88] I have deliberately kept this almost vulgar expression — *L. R.*
[89] Also Mayadevi or Mahamaya — *L. R.*

many nights. No heroic deed can be made against a hero's free will. I am convinced, therefore, that Maya was able to decline the proposal made to her. In case she declined, another woman would give birth to the Buddha. Why, queens are many, the Buddha was only one. Moreover, Maya had many reasons to decline this strange offer. She was only told that her son would become a saint. The very term 'buddha' didn't exist at that time yet. As for bearing a saint, saints were, and still are numerous in India. No-one would be surprised by a new one. And even more: Maya knew that she would pay with her life for the birth of a saint. She didn't even know for certain if she was told the truth or if she was just cheated by powerful demons, let us say. She nursed her child only for a week,[90] she could not know for certain that her baby would become an unsurpassed teacher of man and gods. Nonetheless, she agreed. She agreed to give birth to 'something' greater than herself, to 'something' that had never been before, to someone whose greatness she was never able to realise completely. This is probably the most heroic deed a woman can do.

This doesn't mean that each Buddhist woman ought to bear a saint. It is not only holiness but also novelty that matters. There were women who gave birth to entirely new things. Prajapati Gautami was among them, by the way. She gave birth to the female Sangha. Another woman became the first female lama. No woman had been a lama before her. Nobody knows with certainty who the first female lama was. Two wives of the Tibetan king Songtsen Gampo[91] might be it. These women are also told to be two incarnations of the White and the Green Tara.[92] Whoever it might be, that woman surely was afraid to fail. No man

---

[90] Maya the queen died seven days after the birth of Siddhartha — L. R.

[91] Songtsen Gampo was the 33rd Tibetan king and founder of the Tibetan Empire — L. R.

[92] Tara is a female bodhisattva (deity) in Tibetan Buddhism. She is known as the 'mother of liberation', her role in Buddhism can to some extent be compared to that of Virgin Mary in the Catholic Church — L. R.

was very friendly to her; no man really appreciated her sermons. And yet, she was courageous enough to preach the Dharma. There also was a woman who created a school at which students' intuition, not their logic, was cultivated. I was told about this woman by someone here and am very sorry to forget her name, for she was a European.[93] Don't tell me about the first woman who went to the North Pole. I am not interested in her name.[94] I see absolutely no necessity in going to the North Pole. A man could go there as well, besides. No man could give birth to a buddha, though. No man could become the first female lama. There is a difference between a male and a female lama. A woman believes a female lama more eagerly. I have already told you why even the Buddha wasn't able to create a female religious community. I also think that no man could ever found a school, whose central aim was to foster student's intuition. A man thinks rather logically than intuitively. No man could probably inspire a whole nation to defend its country. I mean France in the middle ages.[95] A man couldn't do it just because men don't really look vulnerable. Defending a man is therefore not very inspiring for a man. I don't mean homosexuals. Homosexuals never go to war.[96] All cases I have mentioned are marked by novelty. By the horror of this novelty. By the greatness of this novelty. Dying in war is not very scary. Being the first female soldier is much more frightening. I think that even today, there may be women whose dreams are disturbed by white elephants; women inspired by great ideas men never realise; by images waiting for their birth; by revelations even these women cannot completely

---

[93] Rinpoche probably means Maria Montessori (1870 – 1952), an Italian physician and educator — *L. R.*

[94] It was Ann Bancroft, by the way — *L. R.*

[95] Rinpoche refers to Joan of Arc whose name he seems to have forgotten — *L. R.*

[96] I probably must say that this is wrong and refer to Alan Turing, an English mathematician (1912 – 1954) or to Sir Hugh Walpole (1884 – 1941). Both were homosexuals. However, Rinpoche's idea is quite clear — *L. R.*

understand; by new thoughts frightening even to them. Some where, a new Maya may live. Or she may be born in some decades.

I named four examples of good Buddhist women. A compassionate courtesan. A nun. A true wife. A heroine. Each example is more precious than the previous one. How can a woman find an opportunity for a heroic deed? Just listen to your intuition. You have this opportunity. Your intuition is stronger than men's.

Ages

We are different. I mean we people of Asia and you Western people are different. One of the biggest lies of your European democracy is the idea of equality of all people. It is, in other words, the idea of universal life standards that are good for everybody. The idea is of course false. There are no universal standards of living that are good for everyone. Even the loftiest religion cannot be the universal good for the whole of mankind. Let alone the standards of living or social regimes. Democracy is neither the best regime nor the only possible one. But now I am not going to talk about democracy.

You probably think we had better not speak about problems and differences. We may pretend there were none. We might pretend to believe that Muslims are similar to Christians; that the things which are good for you are good for them also. So you can attempt to forbid wearing a veil to Muslim women in Paris. It seems to you that wearing a veil humiliates them. Why don't you want these women to decide whether it humiliates them or not? A dispute about wearing a veil is a dispute between religion and politics. I always thought religion to be something more important and noble than politics. Be consistent. Why don't you think that a clean-shaven head humiliates a monk?[97] Does it or does it not? If it does, you ought to punish Buddhist monks who dare walk along your streets. You possibly will do so in some years. Well, I can tell you why you take our shaven heads so easy. It is because we are men. Sexual life is very important for you Western people. As well as for other nations, of course. Only you Westerners regard it as the ultimate good, though. You look for each opportunity to increase your sexual activity. If most of

---

[97] It is a custom for Buddhist monks, especially in the so-called Southern Buddhism, to shave their heads clean — *L. R.*

us were women, you surely would issue a law to forbid us wearing our traditional monastic dress and shaving our heads.

You probably will tell me that a monk has got his free-will to decide what he should wear; that a Muslim woman is, on the contrary, forced to wear a veil by her husband. This is not true, however. She can give up her religion and become one of you Westerners. As well as every one of you can become a Muslim. Or a Buddhist. Most of you European Buddhists want to keep believing in your European lies even *after* taking Refuge. You want to transform Buddhism, to make it convenient to you people of the West. You have already transformed Christianity,[98] now you are going to simplify Buddhism. You want to have an 'easy-going' Dharma that would combine with the lies your society is built upon. I am afraid you won't succeed this way. Buddhism is a religion of Truth.[99] It doesn't combine with lies, however useful they may be.

You will also tell me that a monk may wear any clothes because he is a 'religious professional', unlike Muslim women. This is another big mistake of yours. You always distinguish between laymen and clergy. Why do you want other nations to do it in the same way? We Tibetans can hardly imagine a person beyond any religion. Such an individual is, in our opinion, either mad or vile. Or he is a communist. Well, communism is a religion, too. It is wrong to limit any religion to five per cent of its followers.[100] In doing so you give to the rest of believers no chance of spiritual training. And more than that, in doing so you give up the idea of transforming your society, of making it more just. More Christian-like, so to say. A person who doesn't care for any religion[101]

---

[98] I do not know whether it is true, nor am I in a position to judge — L. R.

[99] Much in the same way all other major religions are, I believe — L. R.

[100] By 'five percent of its followers,' Rinpoche probably meant its clergy – L. R..

[101] Rinpoche clearly means 'a system of beliefs and values' when he uses this word here — L. R.

won't make society better. Such an individual will make money instead. Your 'game rules' allow five per cent of the population to care about religion under condition that these five per cent don't bother anybody, that these people take upon themselves your mutual responsibility for the spiritual improvement of mankind. Well, it is your right to make this mistake. Why did you Christians decide for Muslims how *they* should act, though? In Europe, you have the right to ban all religions except Christianity. I am not joking. Why, it is your fatherland. But be honest. Don't tell, then, that you respect the rights of each minority. The fact is that today, your European homosexuals may do what they want, while your faithful people cannot.

I don't underestimate problems you have with your Muslims. I know that they are doing you much harm. It is Muslim teenagers who keep burning down the cars of Parisians. Deport them from Europe, then. It would be fairer. But you cannot, for you worship Democracy, your idol, and this idol forbids any 'discrimination.' It doesn't forbid discrimination somewhere abroad, though. Deporting Arabs from Paris is told to be discrimination, an assault on human rights. However, you don't regard killing native Tibetans by the Chinese government and forbidding them (*us*, in fact!) to speak their native language as an assault on human rights. You regard it as China's own affair. To be honest, you surely would be much more active in defending the rights of Tibetans if China were not so strong. It is something you call political pragmatism.

But we are not discussing democracy right now. Neither democracy nor political hypocrisy. I just want to emphasise that speaking about problems is more useful than pretending there were none. Having found a problem, we have a chance to find a solution. Pretending to have no problems never solves them. Noticing your problems doesn't mean my unfriendliness to the West. Quite the contrary, I have much sympathy for Europe. I have been living here for twenty years. It is my sympathy for you that allows me to speak about your problems. If I were indifferent to you I surely would tell you that you have none, that Europe is the best part of the world.

I want to tell you about human ages. I am not going to tell you how you Western people perceive us people of Asia. You know it better than me. For you, we are just 'poor folk.' Plain, uneducated persons. Something like 'village idiots'. I am afraid that we perceive you in the same way. Sounds quite insulting for you, eh? Have you never guessed it? Do you want to know why you have never guessed it? It is because we are more friendly. Yes, it is we 'poor folk' of Asia who are more friendly and tactful. If a Tibetan comes to Germany and begins to eat with his fingers in a café, he surely will be criticised. Five of ten Germans will say to him, 'Stop it! Nobody eats by fingers in a café!' Or even more, 'Where are you from, you idiot?' Look here, does the guy do you any harm? Now fancy a drunken German somewhere in a Thai hotel, a drunken German who beats the reception counter with his fists. However, the female receptionist smiles back in a friendly way. The girl is a Buddhist, to begin with. So she smiles to the drunk man in spite of his disturbing her and other hotel guests. She probably regards this drunken German as a pig. She never demonstrates it, though. It is not polite. She won't tell him what she thinks of him, unlike you Western people who start 'opening your sincere mind' about a person after an hour of acquaintance with him or her, except for the cases in which you depend on this person or want him or her to be useful for you. It is a feature you are proud of. The Germans are surely proud of it. The French and the British are more polite. But it depends on their mood. It seems to you that the Thai girl admires you. Why else would she smile? For Heaven's sake, why would she admire you? Her smile is just a fact of her culture. She doesn't want you to suffer seeing her angry face. It is simply compassion! Yes, she *pities* you. And you think her compassion to be admiration. No greater mistake could be ever made.

Look with our Asian eyes at the ages you go through.

You regard the age from birth to twelve years as childhood. We Tibetans don't agree. His Holiness the Dalai Lama[102] may make a political statement at the age of seven. A common Tibetan boy begins to help his father as soon as he can stand erect. No allowances are made for his tender age. However, you believe that a kid shouldn't get in touch with 'the coarse side of this life,' that he or she shouldn't work hard. But in school, of course. As for me, I cannot regard some very dull scholar activities as a good occupation for a kid. A child will certainly detest his or her studies in case his or her head is permanently stuffed with nothing but words, words, words, in case he or she is not allowed to learn real things. He or she will come to detest all professions, in fact. So it is your education system which ruins your society.

It is not only school I speak of. At the age of seven, one already can take serious decisions. One can take Buddhist monastic vows, for instance. But you persuade a seven-year-old person, someone who already can decide, that he or she doesn't live a real life yet, that the real live will come 'in due time.' In ten years, let us say. It is a very dangerous idea. This idea will stay with the person for the length of his or her life.

There are two more things which do your children much harm.

To begin with, it is your 'working' on their shyness. You regard children's shyness as a bad feature. You literally force your kids to be shameless. To argue as soon as they are able to utter words. To form their own opinion on everything. To doubt about everything. To believe in nothing. To respect nobody. One day you will see what it produces.

---

[102] *Dalai Lama* is a title given by the Tibetan people for the foremost spiritual leader of the Gelug or 'Yellow Hat' school of Tibetan Buddhism, and he is often considered to be the supreme head of Tibetan Buddhism in general. The 14th and current Dalai Lama is Tenzin Gyatso — *L. R.*

It is, secondly, cultivating their sexuality.

You will certainly tell me that you don't cultivate it. Well, you don't do it in school.[103] It's something at least. But you allow your mass media to do it. It is your mass media that sexualise children. Magazines, the Internet, TV shows. I remember a scene from a French film the name of which I forgot.[104] A father visits the school his daughter goes to. The girl is seven or eight years old. Her girlfriends see the father and exchange their opinions on his sexual attractiveness. They find him to be very sexy. I am not joking. A scene like that would be impossible in India, in China, in Thailand. It is because we are just 'poor folk,' uneducated people, enemies of democracy who forbid their kids to have their own opinion. Be consistent! May an eight-year-old admire the sexuality of a grown-up man, she also may sleep with him if she wants it. Or may she not? You answer: impossible, she is only a child. Don't be naïve. Prince Rahula[105] became a monk when he was seven. His Holiness the Fourteenth Dalai Lama gave an audience to several Chinese generals and discussed with them the future of Tibet when he was a teenager. Please forgive me for my rudeness, but I don't think that making children is a more difficult occupation than discussing the fatherland's destiny. I simply do not.

Let us go on. Thirteen or fourteen is the age of puberty. A former boy or girl becomes a young man or a young lady. Youth as an age has its own peculiar features. One of them is the belief in ideals. The other is high demands on others. The third one is searching for pleasure.

---

[103] I am sorry to say that this sounds very outdated. Today, we Western nations do — L. R.

[104] I guess it is *La Boum*, a 1980 French comedy film starring Sophie Marceau. I only wonder why Rinpoche would refer to such a relatively harmless scene (it is, harmless in modern terms) — L. R.

[105] Rahula was the only son of Siddhartha Gautama, or the Buddha, and His wife and princess Yashodhara — L. R.

It is not so easy to find some ideals in your Western world, though. For the youth, you have left no ideals intact. It is your education system that destroys all ideals. You teach your children to believe in nothing, to doubt about everything, to analyse everything. It combines with their high demands on other people. Young people neglect mediocrities. For the youth, only two kinds of people exist: heroes and scoundrels. If you aren't a hero, you are a scoundrel for them. It also combines with your modern Western inclination to destroy ideals. It is you Westerners who admire nothing. As a result, your young men and young ladies have no spiritual authorities left. Some of them wanted to admire, say, Catholic priests. But they were told that Catholic priests sleep with boys, and it was you who told them that. So they start to despise Catholicism, as well as any religion in general.

I don't believe all the calumnies told about Catholic priests to be true. I used to hear, or read, a lot of such stories. Do you think it is beneficial to spread them? And what makes you criticise the Church if you are not believers, anyway? Are your social justice warriors not afraid of destroying the church and the family? Back to our subject: what should young men and women believe in? You have persuaded yourselves as well as them that the youth can never be interested in religion. Religion is only for old fogies like me, so you think. It is a great mistake. Not all of my monastic fellow-students had passed final exams and got the degree of Geshe Hlarampa[106]. But their decision to withstand all difficulties and to finally become a doctor of Buddhist philosophy was often taken at the age of fifteen or sixteen. This age often was a turning point for the best of them. I am not going to say that each young man must become a religious leader. However, admiring outstanding individuals, dead or living, religious leaders or not, is as natural for the youth as falling in love with

---

[106] *Geshe* is a Tibetan Buddhist academic degree for monks and nuns. There are four geshe categories, Dorampa, Lingtse, Tsorampa and Lharampa (or Hlaramla, as some older sources have it), Lharampa being the highest — L. R.

someone. You give them no chance to do it, though. A distinguishing feature of Western people is looking for funny or mean peculiarities of great persons. As a rule, only teenagers are inclined to do this. Watch the film *Amadeus*[107] and you will grasp what I mean. For you, it is democracy. You think that it is very funny to show Mozart as a ladies' man. As for me, I absolutely cannot realise how a simple ladies' man could create pieces of music that are, and will be, admired for centuries. You fail to show his moments of inspiration. You are not able to do it. It is because his moments of inspiration will differ him from other people. It is not 'democratic.' It makes other people feel inferior to Mozart. It discriminates among them. But be honest: you certainly had had outstanding persons in your history. And these persons surely differed from the crowd. You don't admit it, though. You say, their genius appeared 'spontaneously,' at random. So you don't think them worth admiring. Nobody is worth admiring for you. Whom should your youth admire if you call Mozart a ladies' man, if you call Wagner[108] the favourite composer of Adolf Hitler, and so on? I don't regard being the favourite composer of Hitler as Wagner's fault. You do. As a result, your youth idolises the so-called stars, the popular singers. It was you who has channeled their aspiration for high ideals into something which is relatively harmless and convenient to you. It is difficult to become disappointed in the Buddha. But one cannot help becoming disappointed in a pop idol. Somebody who still has faith in the ideals he or she used to have when he or she was a young person makes the world a better place. But you don't want to make the world a better place. Your world is the best one for you. Why, you have got your democracy and your mobile phones. What else could one wish to be happy?

---

[107] *Amadeus* is a 1984 American period drama film directed by Miloš Forman. The film's many historical inaccuracies have attracted criticism from music historians — *L. R.*

[108] Richard Wagner (1813–1882) was a German composer, theatre director, polemicist, and conductor — *L. R.*

The youth of Asia search for sensual pleasure as well as the Western youth. But the Asian society prevents physical relations of young people before they get married. On the contrary, you Westerners provide the youth with ample opportunities for sexual contacts. I am convinced that an early sexual experience does much harm to their mental development. You see, even a grown-up person, when overpowered by sexual desires, can scarcely think of something else, so strong they are. The less a young man. How many of us monks would pass the final exams for the Geshe Hlarampa degree if women were allowed to enter monastic colleges? Nobody! Your young men and ladies are not very clever, I say. You smile back ironically. You don't believe me. Because it is you Western people who invented the very best engines. Constructing the very best engines doesn't necessarily require much intelligence, however. A computer can be the best chess player, indeed. But no computer will ever write a Lamrim[109].

And, secondly, do you really think that persons who invented your computers began their sex life when they were fifteen?

From fifteen to twenty-five you are looking for sensual pleasure. For different and strong pleasures. Well for you, if these pleasures do not destroy your brain and do not injure your health. Some of you will stop at the right time.

You stop because you are weary of strong pleasures. At the time Tibetans only begin to live their sex life you already turn away from it. Your middle age begins.

It is good when aspiration for pleasure combines with the physical prime of life. Passions are bad, indeed. But it is passions that let us make decisions. Our decisions change the world we live

---

[109] *Lamrim* (Tibetan 'stages of the path') is a Tibetan Buddhist textual form for presenting the stages in the complete path to enlightenment as taught by the Buddha — L. R.

in. The age of twenty-five is surely the best time for passions. When shall you go for sensual things if not in your prime of life? Surely not when you are a child? And not when you are an old person?

However, you fail to have strong passions at your middle age. It doesn't mean that you become saint. You are just overfed. Your sex life began at the age of fourteen. At the age of thirty, it is no longer something thriving and breathtaking. As a result, you never kill your partner out of jealousy. You never take the wife of your neighbour away by force. You never leave everything to go abroad after your beloved.

I don't mean that killing out of jealousy or taking a woman away by force is all right. However, someone who decides to kill may make better decisions as well. One may decide to adopt a child. To become a musician. To take monastic vows. To marry a woman one will live with until death separates them. You people overfed with passions seldom take serious decisions.

There are three reasons for this.

To begin with, only a saint can make up his or her mind to do something without *any* desire. Desires help decide. But you don't have any strong desires left at your middle age. You are already disappointed in your life.

Secondly, in your childhood, you were persuaded that you would have time to live a 'real' life. So you just prepared to live. Neither had you any time left for a 'real' life in your youth, when you were madly striving for pleasure. Your middle age came, and you didn't still learn how to decide, how to take upon yourselves responsibility for your own decisions.

Your middle age, thirdly, makes many of you depend on the opinion of others.

You see, there is a strange law of mental life. An early slavery leads to the final freedom. An early freedom leads to the final slavery. We Tibetans believe in spiritual authorities at the age of fourteen. As a result, we become clever enough to have an independent opinion at twenty-five. You Europeans cultivate your 'independent thinking' since you are seven. As a result, at the age of thirty you are awfully sick of your 'opinion' which relies on *nothing*. So you start looking for authorities, dead or living. You mentally enslave yourselves. Some of you become Catholics. Others become communists. Others Buddhists. There are many 'isms' to be enslaved by. This is how I look at the European Buddhism. Many of Western Buddhists are not free. Many of them make tremendous efforts to give up their own opinion, to find a lama, their source of the only truth on earth, to idolise him, to repeat all words after him. Every sincere lama tries to prevent such behaviour. Namkhay Norbu[110] surely does. He shocks his followers on purpose. I sometimes do the same. And yet, there *are* people who idolise us. I don't speak about people in this prayer hall. Your ability to stand criticism shows that you are not fanatics, that my general observations are not true or not completely true when applied to you. There are fanatics whose pleasure is being criticised, though.

The simplest way to become mentally dependent on others is your belief in 'public opinion.' Your belief in ideas that are shared by nine out of ten persons. In democracy, for example. Another example is *green world*[111] and protection of environment in general. These ideas are not necessarily false. I have nothing against environmental protection. But, you know, your protests

---

[110] Namkhai Norbu (1938 – 2018) was a Tibetan Dzogchen master — *L. R.*

[111] Rinpoche probably refers to *Greenpeace* or, maybe, to Project Greenworld International, a children's environmental organization, or, again, to *Stromio GmbH*, a German company also known by name of *Grünwelt*, any of which are not to be mixed up with 'the Green World', a term coined by the critic Northrop Frye in his discussion of William Shakespeare's works — *L. R.*

against pollution of the environment are adolescent. The Germans are fighting against new nuclear power plants being built. Do they have another way to produce energy? I don't know. I am not a scientist. They probably do. Wind turbines, for example. Some researchers say that wind turbines do as much harm to the environment as nuclear power plants.[112] It may be so, it may be not. To protest against nuclear stations being built, one should find another solution first, and a good one. Imagine that each nuclear station is stopped tomorrow. As a result, a quarter of all your households will have no electricity. Then you will be the first to call your officials scoundrels. Well, this is very adolescent.

A middle-aged Westerner is a strange person. It is someone who is weary of his or her passions. It is, in a way, an old person. At the same time, it is a child because he or she depends on the opinion of others. It is so because he or she worships public opinion or another mental idol. It is so because he or she refuses to take responsibility upon himself or herself.

Then old age comes.

At this age, you usually become free from your mental slavery, from worshipping idols. You are disappointed in them in the same way in which you formerly became disappointed in passions. Neither do you believe in the so-called 'European values.' At the bottom of your heart you probably wish to believe in something. But it is already too late to begin a new life when you are a senior person. As a result, you become ironical observers. Mockers. Someone who stands aside and says, 'I don't like this.

---

[112] See, for instance, *Wind Energy and Birds* by Michael Hutchins, published on the official website of *American Bird Conservancy* on April 8, 2017 (URL : https://abcbirds.org/wind-energy-threatens-birds/, accessed August 27, 2019). I was unable to detect earlier researches Rinpoche might have read and refer to — L. R.

I don't like that. Everything in our society is bad. I don't know what Good is. No Good has ever existed.'

Another strange peculiarity of your old age is your attempt to preserve your attractiveness, your ability to attract another sex. Some of you want to be loved by women even when they are seventy. Some Western women behave at the age of sixty as if they were twenty. I cannot grasp why you do it. An Indian proverb says that it is bad to die young. In your youth, the soft flesh of your mind is not ripe enough, it cannot be easily separated from the husk of your body. The ripe fruit flesh easily separates from the husk of the mango fruit. But you attempt to remain unripe even when your autumn comes. Why don't you think about your afterlife? Why don't you realise that this afterlife will be painful to anyone who won't grow ripe enough? After the death of your body, your passions will stay with you. You had had a chance to tame them beforehand, but you have never used this chance. So your passions will enslave you. They will possess you and draw you to hell. You are right when you say that it was man who created hell, and this is how it was done.

I don't know whether you agree with my description of ages or not. Why should you listen to me if you think I am mistaken? There is no need of listening to me if you find these strange Western peculiarities of each age all right. However, I hope that some of my listeners rather dislike the idea of being a child in their youth, an old child in their maturity, and an ironical teenager in their senior age. What can you do to avoid it?

You had had to begin in your childhood. In any case, there is only one possibility to avoid the usual Western way of passing ages.

To become an adult, you should go through the stage of a teenager. That of an intelligent teenager, a teenager who believes in good authorities. To say it in other words, you ought to choose a good teaching and to believe in it. Don't follow this teaching as a blind fanatic. Just be friendly towards it. Open your mind for Good you can learn from the teaching. Give up your bad habit to doubt on everything and to believe in nothing.

And then start making decisions. Start taking responsibility for these decisions on yourself. Let these decisions be independent. Let them change your life. Let them be dangerous. You probably tell me that you are able to do it right now. You may be able to do it if you never complain. Even a kid can make a decision. Imagine that a kid decides to play with scissors. But then, having injured himself or herself by the scissors he or she will cry and run to his or her mother. The difference between a child and a grown-up person is that the latter never complains.

The best thing is making decisions without depending on the opinion of others. Listen to nobody but to your conscience. Your conscience will sometimes go against public opinion. To believe in your conscience, you need to have one. You need to have your own true opinion on everything. It can appear only in case you assimilate well a good religious teaching. If you make its ideas to be yours. I don't mean simply learning them by heart, I mean their profound understanding. There is no strict necessity to follow Buddhism. Follow Christianity if you can. But follow if without repeating the old pseudo-Christian lies your society is built on.

Restrict your sensuality, thirdly. You don't need to give it up completely, not yet. Only try to moderate it. Most of you aren't capable of becoming monks. However, desires of a person who restricts his or her sensuality grow stronger and more pure at the same time.

No complaints, belief in a good Teaching, and restricting your sensuality. The first one will tame your hatred, the second one will lessen your ignorance, and the third one will diminish your attachments. When asked which of the three spiritual efforts is the most important one, I answer: the fight with ignorance. Open-mindedness. Ability to learn. Giving up your prejudices. I shall repeat the mental law you already know:

Anyone who begins with freedom ends up by slavery.
Anyone who begins with slavery ends up by Liberation.

Music

Most of you make a grave mistake when you think that the Dharma is limited to books, oral teachings, and meditations. There is no independent self-existing Dharma. Dharma in itself doesn't exist. You are seriously mistaken if you think that the Four Noble Truths[113] or things like them do exist in themselves, by their own force, somewhere in the sky, written on a golden cloud. The Four Noble Truths are only a way to describe the reality which also can be described in another way. I am trying to make you understand that *everything* can be regarded as Dharma. Everything, under condition that it leads you to the Final Liberation. If your job or your daily activity leads you to Enlightenment then your job *is* Dharma. It is said that all deeds of a bodhisattva are Dharma. Even bodhisattva's breakfast or lunch.

And the other way around, if your spiritual practice leads you away from the Final Liberation, this very practice is not Dharma for you, however dharmic it may be for your companion or friend.

Everything I have said right now is also true when applied to the old European music.[114]

The old European music is beautiful.

It wasn't my opinion when I heard it for the first time, in South India, many years ago. Then I rather disliked it. Too many sounds, I thought then. Too perfect. Too fine. Too exalted. Too

---

[113] In Buddhism, the Four Noble Truths are 'the truths of the Noble Ones', the truths or realities for the 'spiritually worthy ones'. They are traditionally identified as the first teaching given by the Buddha, and considered one of the most important teachings in Buddhism — *L. R.*

[114] Rinpoche means classical music of European composers — *L. R.*

idealistic. Of what use are so many sounds?

We Tibetans have a different conception of music, you know. Our monastic music is composed and played just to keep our senses alert. Not to fall asleep, to concentrate on a long prayer. In Tibetan monastic music, there is no need of beauty. It is good as long as it is useful.

But there was something in your music I could not get rid of. Something I could not understand at the first glance. So I started studying it. And when now I say that it is beautiful, it is my honest Buddhist opinion.

I have hardly any doubts that the figure of Jesus Christ is the very origin, the very source of the old European music.

Jesus wasn't a musician. And yet, His figure never ceases to puzzle me. He is your biggest jewel and your greatest enigma. Regarding Jesus as the source of your culture and music, I don't mean your Church music in particular. I mean the idealistic spirit of the Christian teaching.

I feel that I have almost run out of words to explain the birth of your music from the spirit of the Gospel. I will try, though. In fact, I have almost made it to my job, I mean explanation of most inexplicable things almost nobody believes in.

I will begin with *Carmen*, the famous French opera.[115] I laughed when I heard it for the first time. You surely know its plot. A military officer falls in love with a beautiful woman employed at a tobacco fabric. The woman seems to be interested in him for a while, and then she gives her attention to a young bull-killer, a

---

[115] *Carmen* is an opera in four acts by French composer Georges Bizet
— L. R.

toreador. A bull-killer is still a bull-killer by whatever names we call him. Well, the officer murders the woman out of jealousy.

And just think of songs they sing! No bull-killer, no manual worker, and no military man would ever sing this way, even if we imagine that butchers sing at all. Butchers, soldiers, and fabric workers are rude persons, not very fond of sweet songs. So the opera seemed very unnatural to me.

And then, once, I realised one thing. *Carmen* doesn't display the life how it is. It shows the life how it may be.

The lieutenant of *Carmen* isn't a real person. It's an ideal officer, an ideal of a warrior, passionate and gentle at the same time. The opera is filled with ideals. And these ideals come from the spirit of Jesus, the greatest idealist who wanted people to be like angels in the sky. Don't ask for proofs. I have none. I just feel so.

And it's not only *Carmen*. The whole of the nineteenth century music describes the world that doesn't exist yet. Or this world may exist elsewhere. The Universe is a thing we know very little of.

You may ask me, 'Of what use is this ideal world for us poor folk?' Well, it awakens our desire for a better life, gentler, more just, and more beautiful.

There are two ways of reaching Liberation. The Buddhist one is analysis. You look at this world. You look attentively and see how it goes. And then you say: How dreadful! Is *this* a thing I should strive for or be attached to? No, thanks. How beautiful *that one* beyond this loathsome world must be!

The Christian way is dreaming. You look at the picture of Jesus. Or you listen to a beautiful piece of music which shall be said to be a better picture of God than any painting. And you say: How beautiful! How I long for it! How dreadful must this be, this world that never presents such beauty! Shall I be fond of this world? No, thanks. Just listen to some pieces of Chopin, a Polish composer, and you will feel what I mean.

Or shall I love this world, in spite of its being evil? Shall I, when thinking that there are some beautiful sounds this world has created? Look, there was once an ideal officer, and he loved an ideal woman, and he killed her with an ideal knife. There was none, to be honest. The music deceives us, but let the illusion be for the time being, it is a good one. I can try to achieve something as long as I believe in this illusion. I can attempt to live on earth and to be a good person at the same time. The attempt will probably fail. But this attempt will make the world we live in a better place.

And there is much more in the old European music. It goes beyond idealism. It cultivates our fine feelings, our intuition which is something we absolutely need, something we cannot go without on the way to the Final Liberation.

Why is intuition so important? Because it allows us to *see things*. An average European doesn't usually see things. He only sees the words, the labels which other Western people invented to *hide* things. Why was it necessary to hide things? It is because everyone who sees things as they are can also see the lies your society is built on. Your society would crash if a large enough number of people saw those lies.

Is music dangerous for a state? It is. The nineteenth century is the age of glorious music and of two revolutions.[116] The Germans and the French were the best at music at that time. These both nations had suffered from their revolutions. The very

---

[116] Given that there were more than two revolutions in the nineteenth century, it's not clear which two Rinpoche had in mind. – *L.R.*

beginning of the twentieth century still had its great music. The same century faced two world wars.

Now you may well laugh at me and think, 'How absurd! He tries to make us believe it was music that caused world wars.' It was not music in itself. It was the strong desire for a better world, inspired by music. Music cheats. And for a while it makes us believe that a better world exists and that it can be found on earth.

The idea that one can win a better world by a gun will never enter your head if you are intelligent enough. But one cannot become intelligent in an instant. Everything was done to make you silly. Why, you had spent thirteen years in school where you had learnt no real thing, no things but words and concepts. How could you help getting silly after thirteen years of stuffing your head with labels? And now, for a brief moment, you hear a piece of music you have never been taught to understand. It's no wonder that they both come together in your silly uncultivated head, I mean your strong desire for a better world inspired by music and the idea it can be won by taking gun and shooting at your enemies, the idea you probably were taught at school. Then a war starts.

Don't make war. And don't make love either.[117] Learn new things and cultivate your mind instead. First of all, you should forget everything you have learnt in school about music. Everything about code[118], and fugues,[119] and rhythm, and main

---

[117] *Make love, not war* is an anti-war slogan commonly associated with the American counterculture of the 1960s. It was used primarily by those who were opposed to the Vietnam War, but has been invoked in other anti-war contexts since, around the world — *L. R.*

[118] In music, a *coda* (Italian for 'tail', plural *code*) is a passage that brings a piece (or a movement) to an end. Technically, it is an expanded cadence. Just think of the fact that a native Tibetan could learn these very special music terms — *L. R.*

[119] In music, a *fugue* is a contrapuntal compositional technique in two or more voices, built on a subject that is introduced at the beginning in imitation and which recurs frequently in the course of the composition — *L. R.*

themes, and barocco music, and romanticism music and what's-the-name-for-all-this. Then you should simply listen, as if you were a child. You probably will learn something by such listening. Something about yourself. About the world of ideas and ideals. About therapy.

Do you know what I mean by 'therapy'? The therapy of your mind. Music is dangerous. Every poison is dangerous. So music can be poisonous. However, each poison can become a medicine. There is no absolute poison and no absolute medicine as well as no absolute Dharma. So you can cure diseases of your mind, your mental obscurations, by the medicine of music.

If you were attentive enough you would notice the influence of different composers on your mind. You could feel in what direction their music drives you. You would be aware that compassion grows on the soil of Beethoven. That intelligence flourishes in the garden of [J. S.] Bach. That Chopin makes your selfish wishes fade. Here you have three medicines to cut the three roots of Evil, being hatred, ignorance, and attachment. This is what I call therapy. I could also say more about different composers. But will you believe me? Some of you smile ironically and regard this teaching as a fairy-tale. But you do not need to believe me. You must believe your own eyes and ears. And your brain, if you have one.

Listen! Learn how to listen. Learn to appreciate your old music, this precious gem Jesus your Western teacher had left you. The water makes its way through a rock, drop by drop. The invisible sounds of music destroy the rock of your ignorance, little by little.

Lies

Each time I explain the Vinaya[120] to my students, they wonder why we Buddhists count cheating others as one of the main evil deeds. As the deeds like murder, theft, and adultery. You Western people have never regarded cheating as a very grave fault. You say, for instance, that there is a so-called 'white lie' nobody can go without. You even believe that everybody lies. Monks and priests also.

This is your serious problem.

Both your belief that lying never does much harm, and your idea that everybody lies, too.

Your priests are hardly guilty of their lies. You have left them no other choice. But I do think that it was they who created and proclaimed a number of lies your society is built on. What else could they do? They had to choose between the lesser and the greater evil.

Methinks the origin of the problem was Jesus.

Well, right now you are thinking: surely, he cannot go without criticising our religion and our Western teacher. How mean of him. I am not criticising. I am grieving. Jesus is not guilty of those lies. In fact it is you who is guilty. *His* only fault was that He was too unlike you.

You Western people are managers and businessmen. Jesus wasn't. He was a great poet. A dreamer. Now it may seem to you that I am disparaging Him again, because a dreamer is not worth

---

120 The Vinaya is the regulatory framework for the sangha or monastic community of Buddhism based on the canonical texts called the Vinaya Pitaka — *L. R.*

much for you. But this discrediting of dreamers comes from your mind, not from mine. We appreciate dreamers very much. Why, I am one, too. It was very naïve of me to go to Europe in order to spread the Holy Teaching of the Buddha. Only a dreamer is able to be naïve. Well, I don't regret it. Spreading the Dharma in Europe is a direct way to become a bodhisattva. A Ksitigarbha.[121] I hope someone of you understand what I mean.

Jesus was a great dreamer, a great poet, a great idealist. But He was not only a dreamer. I do think He accomplished everything He dreamed of. And He hoped sincerely that everybody will accomplish it, too.

You Europeans called yourselves His disciples. So you had to do something to be like His disciples. Jesus didn't leave any gradual description, any treatise on the stages-of-the-path behind. Poets dislike scientific approach. You can reach Liberation if you walk by steps which are described and numerated in Lamrim. But you can hardly reach the Kingdom of Heaven, as it is called in the Gospel, if you go at a slow pace. It is a jump you need. Or several jumps. The first jump: love your enemies and pray for those who persecute you. Something we Buddhist call *lojong*[122], or developing a good heart. The second jump: go and sell all you have and follow your teacher. Something the Buddha taught to His first disciples.

Those jumps were too hard for most of you. But in fact one can walk only by jumps if he or she follows Jesus. So it was only one

---

[121] *Kṣitigarbha* is a bodhisattva primarily revered in East Asian Buddhism and usually depicted as a Buddhist monk. He is therefore often regarded as the bodhisattva of hell-beings, as well as the guardian of children and patron deity of deceased children — L. R.

[122] *Lojong* is a mind training practice in the Tibetan Buddhist tradition based on a set of aphorisms formulated in Tibet in the 12th century by Chekawa Yeshe Dorje. The practice involves refining and purifying one's motivations and attitudes. In includes such methods as 'Be grateful to everyone', 'When everything goes wrong, treat disaster as a way to wake up', etc. — L. R.

thing left for your priests. To make believe. To pretend to be. To lie.[123] To assure you that you are jumping. Right now. That you are already in the air. That you have good chances to land on the other bank of the river. But in reality, you didn't ever start.

I repeat: what else could they do? Should they say that no-one of you would be like Jesus? There would be no need of religion, then. Then you all would have remained as you had been before. So they *had* to simulate something that wasn't there.

Thus a number of lies were created. And those lies determine your whole life, the life of your Western society. They are something a child is taught first of all.

Now let's look at them more closely.

Lie number one: ideas are more important than human beings.

Lie number two: your society permanently develops, it continually makes progress.

Lie number three: democracy is the best regime.

Lie number four: your wealth depends on your moral qualities. It depends on how good you are.

Lie number five: the eternal love between man and woman does exist.

Lie number six: men and women differ from each other neither mentally, nor spiritually.

Lie number seven: things are the same as words we use to call these things.

---

[123] This is, of course, a doubtful way to see Christianity. — *L. R.*

Lie number eight: bad people are rare in your society. And they are always punished for their bad deeds.

Lie number nine: you all are Christians.

We have no time to discuss each of these lies. Democracy is a thing I already told you about. I will discuss only some of them.

Let us begin with the first lie. There are ideas that are more important than individuals. Well, I don't argue. It's true. As for me, ideas like the Four Noble Truths are in fact more important than lives of some individuals. But it does *not* mean that we may kill those individuals in order to spread these ideas. No true idea can be preserved or spread by doing harm to living beings. It is something you have never believed in. And more than that: you have ever thought that people can and should be made good by force. It is absolutely impossible. Violence leads to hatred. Even the best ideas become loathsome to us if we are taught them against our free will. Forcing people to be good is as silly as forcing a river to flow or a tree to grow. Why are you so sure your ideas are good, besides? Your idea of democracy, for example, which you spread by force. You count everybody who doesn't believe in your democracy as scoundrels. Well, we Tibetans as a nation should be called scoundrels, too.

I think it might be the Gospel which inspired you to force other people to be good. Please recall: Jesus went into the Temple of Jerusalem and drove out all the salesmen, and overturned their tables. He did it by force. So you decided you could imitate Him. But how can you know that He had never regretted it afterwards, that He had never been sorry for this deed? Only a statue is never sorry. A living person may be, indeed. I like Jesus for His being human, not for His being an unmistakable God which in fact can never exist.[124] You see, violence always produces violence. This is karma. There were some Jews who wanted Jesus to expel salesman from the temple. There were some who didn't. And the latter grew so angry with Him that they killed Him. It also seems possible that the very people who accompanied Him in the Temple killed Him afterwards because of His being 'too meek' and because of His refusal to head a new revolt against the Romans. This is how the law of karma came true. You may contradict me, you may tell that Jesus was a god and was surely right, forcing someone. But even gods meet the results of their deeds.

There were attempts at the Buddha's life, too. However, His killers had never succeeded, because He carefully avoided violence. (Please don't think that I am juxtaposing the Buddha and Christ in order to disparage the latter.) Maudgalyayana, one of His closest disciples, produced once or twice a miracle wanting some monks to stop their idle talks. But even then free choice was left to these monks. They weren't expelled from the Sangha by a rope. This is how you should behave. You should use force only if you absolutely cannot go without it. You may even kill a criminal if his death saves many lives.[125] But you do think differently. You still believe in the old lie that ideas are more important than human beings. That the former allows killing the latter.

And it is not necessarily killing you praise. You believe that shyness is bad. This is an idea of yours, and you believe that ideas can be spread by force. So you positively force your teenagers not to be shy. I didn't believe it before I had learnt it from one of you. There are special courses in your schools, and the teachers in those courses teach girls and boy how to overcome their shyness. You do so much harm to these girls and boys! A shameless

---

[124] For a Christian, the idea of Jesus being only human is, of course, unacceptable — L. R.

[125] ...But then, having lynched someone, you will have to face prosecution. Just in case — L. R.

girl is not pretty for a young man. I know very well that it sounds 'patriarchal' and is far from being 'politically correct,' yet it is true, however discriminating or 'misogynic' it may sound. Nobody looks at her because she is manlike. Love cannot be compelled. So she thinks all men to be idiots and becomes a lesbian. And vice versa: girls dislike shameless guys. And the guys become homosexuals.

Let us consider the second lie. Society permanently develops, it continually makes progress. But, to tell you the truth, I see no proofs for it. Well, you may call me a close-minded foreigner. Yet methinks that your society did develop, that it had reached its highest point about the middle of the nineteenth century, at the time your best books and your best music were written. And you know, books and music don't display the level of social development by themselves. It is the level of compassion that matters. When I am reading Charles Dickens I do think that you will never gain back that intense compassion and sympathy his heroes and heroines had for each other.

Today, only industry and electronics are making progress. And here is another lie you believe in. You believe that machinery helps you, that machines are your friends. Just believe me that machine guns our monks were killed with were not great friends of humanity.

Each society has its own third *varna*: its *Vaishyas,* the merchants. People who are fond of money and know how to let them grow. Merchants are numerous. But everybody cannot be a businessman. And you still believe that everyone can and should become one. You have ever tried to convince your warriors, your officials, and your priests that they should make money. Now they are convinced. And they do try to make money now. Someone of them is successful. Someone else, someone who didn't yet forget how to preach or how to do properly one's own official duty, is not.[126] You cannot preach and make much money, or teach and make much money, or run a school and make much money at the same time. But your officials, teachers, and priests don't guess it. Finally, they start to regard themselves as losers. Women don't like losers. Women look around and see only 'losers,' because women believe in the fourth lie, too. They think there are no 'real men' anymore. Then they start to do what men used to do before. They become manlike. This is why so many lesbians appear. And the other way around: men dislike manlike women. They look for someone who appreciates them. This is why homosexuals exist.

There also are men who want their 'compensation'. They suffer from being losers and getting little money, so they want their compensation: sexual contacts with many women. And now the fifth lie matters.

Realise that there is no eternal love between man and woman. An eternal compassion *does* exist. An eternal 'romantic' love does not. Jesus' love might be eternal. Jesus needed no women, though. And you Christians pretend to be like Him. Or quite close to Him, at least. But you aren't.

Western girls used to regard the marriage as the main goal of their life. (They don't do it now, of course.) They awaited from their husbands something one awaits from God. There are few gods among men. Those exaggerated hopes made them feel disappointed. Men cheat, a woman thinks. They are not gods. We are much better. This is another way how lesbian love appears. Men are in reality neither better nor worse than women. They just *differ* from women. Men and women are *different*, not only

---

[126] One finds a parallel thought in *Dostoevsky: Language, Faith and Fiction* by Rt Revd Rowan Williams: 'The point at which the activity of nursing the sick can be expressed in terms of a producer supplying a customer is the point at which the culture of nursing the sick begins to disappear' (Rowan William. *Dostoevsky: Language, Faith and Fiction*. London: Continuum, 2008) – L. R.

physically. There are a good number of ideas men are interested in, and women aren't. And vice versa. But a Western woman thinks of a man as of somebody who is like her. And looking at him this way, she surely finds him worse. A man cannot bear a child. He seldom is very handsome. He sometimes has no intuition at all. This is all true. Nonetheless, judging a man by his beauty or his ability to bear children is like comparing a horse and a motorbike. A motorbike is surely faster than a horse. Will you prefer a bike to a horse just because of that? I won't. School teachers do much harm to their students by equalising men and women. They make both genders unhappy. They increase the number of lesbians and homosexuals. But you Europeans find homosexuals all right, don't you? You gave them the same rights everyone in your society has, didn't you? We Buddhists didn't. We never allowed manlike women and womanlike men to take monastic vows.[127] If the Buddha lived today you would accuse Him of discrimination of sexual minorities and bring Him to prison.

A married man in your society finds a mistress instead of marrying two women. He cannot marry two women, unlike us Tibetans, because you do believe that only one eternal love exists. So he feels guilty when falling in love with someone else. You all feel guilty when you recall your childhood and sermons you listened to. (Did you, actually?) You were told that you should be rich, should have only one eternal love of your life, should love everybody in the same way in which the Buddha and Christ did. But you feel that you cannot. This is why you are angry with your religion. This is why so few of you Western people go to church nowadays. Don't misunderstand me. I don't say that marrying many women is all right. The fewer the better, and being a monk is better still. But having many wives is better that

---

[127] Rinpoche probably refers to the fact that according to the scriptures Buddhist monastic vows cannot be taken by hermaphrodites, transsexuals, eunuchs, cross-dressers, and effeminate gay men. This rule is very old but, of course, still valid — *L. R.*

having many mistresses. A man cares for his wife. But he easily leaves a mistress. Or even kills her. Remember *Carmen*. *Carmen* is a European opera. An officer kills a pretty woman because she picks up another lover. Of course, things like that happen in Tibet, too. But we are different in this sight. We admit that people can be overcome by hatred, ignorance, and lust. These roots of evil are bad, but they exist, and it is difficult to get rid of them instantly. Somebody can take monastic vows. But every layman cannot. So we try to bind human lust and jealousy by bonds of morality and tradition. And you count yourselves as angels. You say you will never ever desire another woman. It is because such a desire contradicts the ideal of the eternal love. You think it is not a 'Christian' desire. You pretend to have none. And then, it suddenly rises and destroys your life.

Now look at the seventh lie.

You believe that things are the same as words. That a word always shows the very essence of a thing it labels. A written word in particular. If you studied Prajña Paramita you would realise that it is not true. I think it is your religion which makes you believe it. Have you ever read the very beginning of John's Gospel? *Before the world was created the Word already existed: it was with God, and it was the same as God.* I don't argue with the Gospel. There is a difference between The Word of the Gospel and words we use. Your whole education system is built on words, terms, and concepts. You feel helpless without words. As soon as an original thinker or preacher appears, you try to categorise him. This is what you do first: you look for a label. You think that labels explain things. Now here are some examples of labels invented by you: Plato was an idealist. Or: Jesus was an idealist. Or: Buddhism is a philosophy, not a religion. But these labels explain nothing! Nothing at all. Well, Jesus was an idealist, and you think that idealism is bad. So was Jesus bad? Is your religion bad? Be consistent. Why aren't you?

I ask you why you never analyse things like that. Someone has called Buddhism a philosophy, you have read it and believe that now you know everything about Buddhism. Bud have you ever tasted the Dharma? Do you know its taste? Surely not. Be honest. And who was that who said that Buddhism is not a religion? Don't we Buddhists have our temples? Our preachers? You just find Buddhism not similar to your own religion. So you declare that Buddhism is simply a philosophy. Thinking like this is convenient to you. It is because philosophy determines only the way one thinks, not the way one acts. Philosophers are harmless. They never mind the rich to be rich, the poor to be poor. But you are   mistaken. The Dharma determines our whole life, not only the way we think. This is why Buddhism is a religion. Your professors of religious studies are mistaken in the same way you are.

You Western people, the Germans in particular, always believe in titles. You believe in titles like 'professor,' 'priest,' 'teacher,' and 'physician.' You probably think that the very fact of labelling a person as 'professor' makes one wise. Tell me: why? In a similar way, you believe that your teachers always teach their students what is Truth and Good, just because they are teachers. They have their diplomas. Paper never lies. It was time when your Western teachers taught you that our planet is as flat as a table. And you believed them then as much as you do now, because those teachers had their diploma also. You seem to forget your own school and your feeling of anguish you had when you attended it. It was a shock for me to learn how many of you sincerely disliked your schoolteachers. If you don't like your schoolteachers why do you go to school at all? I tell you: because you cannot help going to school. You are persuaded that each person certified as a teacher is a genuine teacher. That education is always beneficial. And you Western people have ever attempted to bring other people to Good. Even by force. Even if others don't like this 'Good' of yours at all. It is your distinguishing feature. The naivety of European adults strikes me. It is the naivety of people who are able to forget their school boredom and start believing in a good school. But I don't believe that you are so naïve. You just pretend to be naïve. If you permitted yourselves to understand that your education system is bad, then you *would have to do* something. But what? You have never studied pedagogy before, what then? Criticising teachers is easy, but do you know how to educate children, to awaken their sense for Good? Even if you attempted to teach them you should repeat the old lies your society is built upon.

The result of your habit of providing each thing with a label is that you seldom see reality beyond your words. You regard as an educated person someone who knows all your words and terms, not somebody who knows things. A person who had read all your books about Good and Evil is a good priest for you. Not someone who *feels* what is Good and what is Evil. Our lamas also read books. But they are compelled to see things beyond words. If they don't, they won't pass their exams in a *shedra*.[128] But they surely will pass them in a Western university and get a degree.

To sum it up, you believe in your priests, teachers, and professors. But at the very bottom of your heart, you feel that so many of them repeat the old lies, some of which I named. So you turn away from your education and from the educated people. You say: the intellectual life is not real life. I prefer to live real life. This is what you say. Sports or having a mistress are 'real' to your taste. Your women dislike overeducated persons either. But almost everybody is well-educated today; almost everybody has stuffed one's own head with words and terms. How can a woman find a real man among such folk? One more reason for homosexuality to flourish.

And, after all, your final lie. The lie that you are Christians, i.e. followers of Jesus. Well, if being a follower of a teacher means

---

[128] A Buddhist monastic college — *L. R.*

doing the contrary to what the teacher says — then you are Christians, of course. I think that Antichristians are Christians, in a way. A ram is to some extent opposite to a sheep. It is because a sheep is shy and obedient, not like a ram. You call yourselves sheep of Jesus, the Shepherd. But in fact you are like rams that run across fields and never mind the shepherd. Well, a ram is still closer to a sheep than a goat. The trouble is that you Europeans start studying Eastern religions. As a result, you don't know who you are anymore. Neither goat nor sheep. *Ra me lug me.*[129]

What should you do to get rid of your lies? You know the answer. Shall I say it once again?

Stop believing in words. Words are not the same as things. Words are spoken by people. People lie. Stop believing in lies. Close your ears for anything others say to you. Believe nobody. Not even me. Why should you believe me if you don't understand me, and what for? Faith combined with lack of understanding produces fanaticism.

Stop pretending to be a sugarcane[130] saint. You are not Jesus. Not yet. You are not able to love everybody right now. You are not obliged to have one eternal love of your life — which, of course, does not mean that you may break your marriage vows. Being rich isn't necessarily your duty. It is not your fault that you don't understand women, and that they don't understand you. You are not allowed to force anybody to be good. How dare you if you don't ever know what Good is?

---

[129] A Tibetan proverb which means 'neither fish nor fowl' or, literally, 'neither goat nor sheep' — L. R.

[130] The *sugar-cane* bodhicitta is an important term in Tibetan Buddhism. Its meaning varies from 'aspiration of a beginner' to 'a not very sincere religious motivation' — L. R.

And then go to things. Go somewhere people aren't stuffed with words. Go there, and try to find out your own value. Diagnose your obscurations. Try to find a doctor for them. I mean a lama, of course. But don't stay simply waiting for him. Take your sword of meditation and fight the snakes of obscurations that live in the garden of your mind under the leaves of lies.

This is a Buddhist way to Liberation. I suppose that there is a Christian one also. A way where you have to jump over a big gulf. You might grow your wings after you have jumped. But if I were you I would look for a master of jumping first of all. I don't think you can find such a master in every church. Methinks I know the way how to distinguish between a real master and a person who only speaks of jumping.

A master doesn't lie. He who lies won't survive his first jump.

The Buddha and Christ

Today, on the day of the Buddha's Parinirvana, I am going to speak about two great religious teachers, probably the greatest religious teachers the world history has ever seen. I mean the Buddha and Jesus Christ.[131]

Naming them both, I am not going to insult other religions. Mohammad, Krishna, or Zoroaster might be great teachers also. However, their biographies seem to be everything but accurate. One can hardly believe in Mohammad's riding to the sky on the back of a sacred white horse or in Krishna's conquering a demon as big as a mountain, even if one is a faithful person. I want to warn you against despising old legends. Mohammad's sacred horse could be the horse of spiritual discipline. The demon as big as a mountain shouldn't necessarily be a monster like these we see in American movies. Lust, hatred, or ignorance can be as big as a mountain, too. But it seems difficult to distinguish facts from metaphors in the life of Krishna or Mohammad. This is why we had better avoid speaking about them.

On the contrary, the 'biographies' of the Buddha and Christ are quite accurate. We know much about their true lives. It is exactly why we hardly can help admiring their personalities.

In any case, I am far from the idea of inspiring love for them by force. Each Christian has the right not to love the Buddha. But it is simply impossible, even for a Christian, not to respect Him, if one learns the greatness of the Buddha's ideas, His service to humanity, and the immensity of His impact on the whole of Asia. Some Buddhists smile when they look at the sentimental and

---

[131] Rinpoche normally referred to Christ as 'Jesus', however, he also occasionally used 'Christ'. It seems that for him the two words were interchangeable — *L. R.*

sugary idol of Jesus created by the modern Western world.[132] Nonetheless, we cannot help respecting Him for His immense influence on Europe. Without Him, neither your music, nor your architecture, nor your poetry would appear. Of course, you would have some music or architecture even without Christ. But without Him they would be quite different. They would be similar to what the ancient Roman Empire had had as its art. Or they probably would be similar to the modern American music and architecture.[133]

Right now the West faces the fight between two cultures, being the ancient culture that existed before the birth of Christ and the Christian one. The United States of America nowadays is quite the same as the ancient Roman Empire had been. A small bit of the sentimental cult of 'Jesus the sugar boy' makes the only difference.[134] But even this small bit is beneficial. This cult is something like a leash of silk for a terrible beast. The leash is very thin, however, even a thin leash for the beast is better than no leash at all. I hope you understand what I mean. I hope, too, that nobody of you worships the U. S. as an ideal country of freedom. There still are a large number of young persons in France and Germany who do it. You know, I am not going to speak much about America. Not because I am afraid of someone. Just because a monk shouldn't speak much about politics.

---

[132] 'Christ is one of the "family" now. I often wonder if God recognizes His own son the way we've dressed him up, or is it dressed him down? He's a regular peppermint stick now, all sugar-crystal and saccharine when he isn't making veiled references to certain commercial products that every worshipper absolutely needs' (Ray Bradbury, *Fahrenheit 451*). I have never discovered whether Rinpoche was familiar with this novel — L. R.

[133] This paragraph initially included seven more sentences containing Rinpoche's critical observations on the American spirituality. I am sorry to say that Rinpoche had not much respect for the United States of today. A prejudice as it may be, it was a part of his world-view. Having carefully reread those lines I decided that they are more biased than really true. This is why I finally removed them from this chapter — L. R.

[134] I am confident that this is not true or, at least, not completely true — L. R.

Let us go back to the Buddha and Christ. A Buddhist cannot help admiring the Buddha as well as a human being cannot help breathing. I must tell, too, that since my childhood my great devotion for the Buddha was mixed up with astonishment. I admired the Buddha because He was not like other persons who surrounded me. I don't mean His being a saintly man, for He was not like other saints. For a long time, I was trying to grasp: What is it that distinguishes Him from other religious leaders of Asia? I realised it only after my arrival to Europe.

The Buddha is a European.

I don't mean His nationality. There is, in fact, a Western lama[135] who seriously states that the Buddha's forefathers lived in the area of what now is the Ukraine.[136] This lama says it every time he visits the Ukraine. When he visits Germany he probably says that the Buddha's forefathers lived in Germany. The Buddha's national origin doesn't matter much. Even in case the Buddha's forefathers came from the West they got mixed with the Indian people, or peoples. When saying that the Buddha is a European I mean something quite different.

We Tibetans are more dreamers than practical persons. For many centuries, many of us preferred praying in a temple to ploughing soil. A large number of Tibetans still like meditation more than manual labour. Over the centuries, we produced outstanding spiritual treatises and failed to build a regular army.

Indians are even more dreamers than we are. The same is also true of the Nepalese, the Bhutanese, the Thai – in short, for almost all peoples of Asia. We all are dreamers. The only exception is the Japanese. However, Japan is situated so eastwards that one

---

[135] Rinpoche probably refers to Ole Nydahl (born 1941), a Danish lama in the Karma Kagyu school of Tibetan Buddhism − *L. R.*

[136] I am at a loss whether one must keep the article in 'the Ukraine' or leave it out nowadays − *L. R.*

hardly makes out whether it is the Far East or the Far West. Besides, a sea folk as the Japanese are cannot help being industrious, for they have to struggle for their life.

The Buddha is not a dreamer. This distinguishes Him from most of our saints, gurus, and *siddhas*[137].

If Krishna, or Sathya Sai Baba[138], or one of the eighty-four *mahasiddhas*[139] were in the Buddha's place, any of them most likely would decide that there was no need to leave his palace and his family, that Liberation could be achieved within the palace. Why, there is no difference between samsara and Nirvana, as the popular saying goes.[140] This is precisely the point of view of Hashang Mahayana[141], a famous guru from China who was defeated in the well-known dispute with Kamalashila.[142]

The Buddha went another way. He left His palace and His family. He, like Ulysses of the ancient Greece, wandered for many years. He searched for a guru. And He found some, too. But His gurus were all dreamers. And these dreamers preached that for a spiritual practitioner, nothing is to be done.[143] That Liberation

---

[137] A *siddha* in Indian religions and culture means 'one who is accomplished.' It refers to perfected masters who have achieved a high degree of physical as well as spiritual perfection or enlightenment — L. R.

[138] Sathya Sai Baba (1926—2011) was an Indian guru and spiritual leader — L. R.

[139] By convention there are eighty-four *mahasiddhas*, or 'realised practitioners', in both Hindu and Tibetan Buddhist traditions — L. R.

[140] Please see the commentary by Khenpo Tsultrim Gyamtso Rinpoche on *Madhyamakaavatara* by Candrakirti for further reference — L. R.

[141] Hashang Mahayana (8th century) was Chinese Zen master who debated with and was defeated by Kamalashila — L. R.

[142] Unlike many other Buddhist teachers Rinpoche didn't support very much the idea that 'there is no difference between samsara and nirvana', in other words, that there is no difference between this mundane world and the state of eternal bliss. He even went so far as to ascribe this famous saying to the notoriously known Hashang Mahayana for which I could find no textual evidence. While admitting that this maxim may be true from a philosophical point of view, he clearly stated that is very erroneous in terms of practical ethics. — L. R.

[143] I believe this expression can be understood both as 'you don't need to do anything' and as 'nothing can actually be done' — L. R.

is within us. To achieve it, one has simply to stop everything, to desire nothing, to renounce all desires, to realise this very idea that nothing is to be done, and to become enlightened in an instant this way.

Nonetheless, the Buddha had never stopped. He kept going to His goal, and He reached it after defeating Mara over the night of His Enlightenment. While struggling with Mara, He acted as a warrior, not as a priest. A brahman never fights. Each European has something of a warrior. Of our saints, the Buddha and Padmasambhava[144] are warriors, I may say. And *this* is why the Buddha is a European.

It is not only the battle with Mara which matters. For the rest of His life, for forty-five years, in fact, the Buddha had never acted as a common guru. He acted as a manager of a huge enterprise. He didn't think Himself too 'saintly' to retire from many everyday activities of the monastic community. For instance, He ordered to build toilets for monks and devised their plans. Can you ever imagine Milarepa[145] caring for toilets for his followers? Milarepa is precious to us Tibetans because he is a dreamer and a poet, someone like us. The Buddha is loved by us Asian people because He is not like us. He is a hard worker. It is this sense in which I call Him a European.

Please do not think that managers are of more importance than poets. It's wrong. Are you people of the West not yet weary of your contemporary civilisation that has only managers and lacks poetry so much? Don't underestimate managers, though. You see, it is easy to admire a poet. Poetry is beautiful. Religious poetry is even more beautiful than lay poetry. Before Buddhism, any religious text in Asia was pure poetry. One loves to listen to

---

[144] Padmasambhava was an 8th-century Buddhist teacher from the Indian subcontinent — L. R.

[145] Milarepa (1028 – 1111), a Tibetan siddha, is considered as one of Tibet's most famous yogis and poets — L. R.

such poems as the *Bhagavad-Gita*[146] again and again. Toilets are far less beautiful. But they are of great use, too. They are very necessary. Someone voluntarily chooses to work on constructing toilets instead of writing a poem about the White Horse of spiritual discipline, which occupation he would like much more, and this is, in my opinion, a heroic deed.

Having learned more about Jesus, having read the Gospel, I, too, was greatly astonished.

The Buddha, the great teacher in the mainland of dreamers, is a practical man. Jesus, the great teacher in the mainland of practice, is a dreamer.

You don't agree with me, do you? Take your Gospel, then, and reread it. Many deeds of Jesus are not very pragmatic. A practical person would not create food out of nothing, in a miraculous way, for the crowd of his students. A good manager would care for food in advance. Consider the fact that the Buddha never created food out of nothing for thousands of His monks. A manager would not turn water into wine, because he could buy the wine in advance if he absolutely couldn't go without it.[147] Or he would get it as a donation in case of his being a non-profit-manager. A businessman wouldn't ask his disciples to buy a sword just to tell them at the very moment they were going to make use of it that they needed no swords because of thousands of heavenly protectors.[148] I wonder if a businessman can have spiritual

---

[146] The *Bhagavad-Gita* (literally 'The Song of God') is a 700-verse Sanskrit scripture that is part of the Hindu epic Mahabharata. It is the best known and most famous of Hindu sacred texts — L. R.

[147] Rinpoche refers to the wedding at Cana of Galilee where Jesus transformed water into wine according to the Gospel of John (John 2:1-11). This very pragmatic idea of purchasing the wedding wine in advance should be properly understood in the light of Rinpoche's humour, the Western pragmatism being probably the aim of his satire — L. R.

[148] 'Then said Jesus unto Peter, Put up thy sword into the sheath: the cup which my Father hath given me, shall I not drink it?' (John 18:11, KJV) The 'heavenly protectors' are, of course, Rinpoche's own interpretation — L. R.

disciples, by the way. A down-to-earth administrator wouldn't appoint a potential traitor as a community accountant simply to give him a chance of getting better.[149] All these deeds lack realism. Only a great poet could have done them. Please remember that we Asians admire poets.

As soon as I had realised the fact I asked myself: Why was it so? Both the Buddha and Christ could definitely choose where to be born. They certainly could. What was the reason for their paradoxical choices? There surely *was* a good reason, for the East accepted the Buddha as its greatest religious teacher in the same way in which the West accepted Jesus as its only God.

I have grasped this reason only short ago.

Imagine that the Buddha were born in the West! His Teaching would be understood instantly. He wouldn't make tremendous efforts He made in India in order to spread His Teaching among you Westerners. Why, it would seem very familiar to you. 'Work on yourself and be attentive' — this slogan is the easiest way to explain Buddhism. You people of the West would like it very much. You have been doing it for ages. Well, not doing exactly *that*. You work on anything *but* on your own mind. And yet, the Buddha's Teaching is very pragmatic, very scientific. One should never give any pragmatic teaching into the hands of businessmen. They will drive it to the extreme. They will elaborate a business plan to successfully sell it to some losers, and that will be the end of it. They are already doing it.[150] Read some books written by Western lamas. These books contain only ready-made receipts. Draw nine deep breaths through your right nostril, draw nine deep breaths through your left nostril, then meditate

---

[149] Rinpoche refers to Judas Iscariot who according to the Gospel of John carried the disciples' money bag or box (John 12:6) — *L. R.*

[150] I cannot help saying that this is very true. See, for instance, *McMindfulness: The Marketing of Well-Being* posted in *Psychology Today* on June 13, 2014 by Jeremy D. Safran — *L. R.*

on Vajrakilaya[151], and you surely will become enlightened. Enlightenment guaranteed. If not, you will get a refund. These receipts of Western lamas are very different, though, so that one excludes another. Should people achieve different enlightenments by following these different teachings? I don't know. I have never used those ready-made receipts. Neither should you. I don't regard our Buddhist Teaching as fast food.

Now consider the teaching of Jesus, the great dreamer. His teaching was a hard stroke to you Western people. It was something like a beast that all of a sudden started speaking in human voice. You still cannot realise it. How could you, indeed! Jesus told you practical persons that from now on, you should become dreamers. He asked you not to store up riches here on earth.[152] How can a businessman help storing up his riches? Most of you pretended not to hear this sermon. However, some of you did hear it. Some people of the West became saints, something that had never happened before.[153] You got your saints, your dreamers, and your poets. And it was they who softened your cruel Western world a bit. Remember what I said before about a silk leash for the beast. Without your saints and poets, your life here would be unbearable.

Quite the same happened with our mainland, with Asia, when the Buddha was incarnated among us dreamers. We began to work. We started turning the wheel of our attention.[154] And, while turning that wheel, we understood that inventing a

---

[151] *Vajrakilaya* in Tibetan Buddhism is the yidam deity who embodies the enlightened activity of all the buddhas and whose practice is famous for being the most powerful for removing obstacles — L. R.

[152] 'Lay not up for yourselves treasures upon earth, where moth and rust doth corrupt, and where thieves break through and steal' (Matthew, 6:19, KJV) — L.R.

[153] Some historical or, maybe, pseudo-historical texts (see, for instance, *A Letter from Hadrian Augustus to Servianus the Consul*) mention 'Christians' existing before Christ. However, this is a very complex issue that must be handled critically — L. R.

[154] 'Turning the wheel' is a traditional Buddhist metaphor for different religious activities, mainly for preaching — L. R.

windmill, a potter's wheel, or other machines might be of use for us as much as meditation.

Alas, we Tibetans didn't succeed in becoming warriors! Even the Buddha, the glorious prince, wasn't capable of inspiring courage and pride into us. We Tibetans were conquered by the Chinese who kept in touch with you Westerners and had learnt something from you. We couldn't defeat the Chinese army. However, we were able to defeat the Chinese version of Buddhism. Chinese Buddhism is a religion without the Buddha.[155] Chinese Buddhism is pure reverie, pure poetry, dissolution in the Ultimate Nothing. The Buddha never recommended us to dissolve in nothing. Quite the contrary: He advised us to get seven precious gems of a *cakravartin*[156]. The precious horse, the precious elephant, the precious wife[157], the precious counsellor[158], the precious sword[159], the precious jewel, and the precious wheel. Do you know what these seven gems really are? No, you don't. The precious elephant is the elephant of *sopa*, patience.[160] The precious horse, completely tamed by the rider, is the horse of *tshultim*, discipline. The precious wife is the wife of *jinpa*, generous giving that softens our mind. The precious counsellor is the counsellor of attention. The precious sword is the sword of *sherab*, wisdom. The precious wheel is the ever-turning wheel of *tsondu*, joyful enthusiasm. The precious jewel is the jewel of *samten*, concentration nothing is to compare with.

Imagine what would happen if Jesus were born in Asia! We certainly would admire and worship Him, the great poet. And

---

[155] A very doubtful statement, and yet, the concept of *wu wei*, literally meaning 'inexertion' or 'inaction', plays the central role in Chinese Buddhism — *L. R.*

[156] A *cakravartin* in Buddhism is a world conqueror and ideal universal ruler who rules ethically and benevolently over the entire world — *L. R.*

[157] Or 'the precious queen' (Sanskrit *striratna*) — *L. R.*

[158] Or 'the precious minister' (Sanskrit *purusharatna*) — *L. R.*

[159] Or 'the precious general' (Sanskrit *khadgaratna*) — *L. R.*

[160] Rinpoche interprets the seven mythological emblems of royalty as cardinal Buddhist virtues. This interpretation is quite unique — *L. R.*

having accepted Him and His Teaching, we most likely would spend another two millennia sitting in padmasana[161] and dreaming of the Kingdom of Heaven.

This is why each religion is good on its proper place. His Holiness the Dalai Lama the Fourteenth is a bit anxious about spreading Buddhism in the West. Do you understand now what it is he is afraid of? He is afraid of your turning Dharma centres into spiritual supermarkets. I visited many Dharma centres in Europe. I must say that he is quite right in his anxiety. Why, some of you have even succeeded in converting churches into offices and shops,[162] and this despite the character of Christianity, founded by an absolute dreamer. Are you not afraid of what will become of Buddhism in your pragmatic hands? Well, if you learn how not to regard the Buddha as a 'superboss' or as simple medicine from every malady, if you have genuine respect for Him, if you study the Buddha's Teaching carefully and attentively, you will finally become Buddhists. You might be even better Buddhists than we are. It is because you are accustomed to work hard. You are laborious people. You only have to channel your energy into work on your own selves. This labour is difficult, too. It requires as much qualification and effort as the kind of work you are used to.

---

[161] *Padmasana* or lotus position is a cross-legged sitting position originating in meditative practices of ancient India, in which each foot is placed on the opposite thigh — L. R.

[162] I am uncertain whether Rinpoche meant it figuratively or literally. An easy search on Google would provide you with numerous recommendations on 'how to convert a church into a home' — L. R.

Intuition

You possibly know what emptiness of all things[163] really is. Things are empty of their being in an absolute, ultimate way. From their being pure abstract ideas. They exist interdependently. It means things don't exist independently from other things.

Those of your who have studied the Cittamatra[164] philosophy know that there are different kinds of emptiness. There also are two extremes we are inclined to fall into. The first extreme is the idea that the nature of concepts is as essential as that of things. The second extreme is the idea that the nature of things is as deceptive as that of concepts.[165]

What is a concept? It is an idea, a term. A word, if you wish. A sign. Consider the concept of a table. While believing that there really is a table which exists absolutely, and independently from the people who think these four wooden legs and a desk to be a table — while believing this we follow the first extreme. When believing that the very wood of the table is a convention, an illusion, we follow the second one.

All students of our Buddhist College must know it very well. But it is not so obvious for others. You probably will ask me: is this a problem? Especially when we think of the world finance crisis, of prostitution, of narcotics that come to Europe from the Middle

---

[163] Emptiness (Sanskrit *śunyata*) is a Buddhist concept which has multiple meanings depending on its doctrinal context. In Mahayana Buddhism it usually refers to the tenet that all things are empty of intrinsic existence and nature (svabhava) — *L. R.*

[164] *Cittamatra* is an influential tradition of Buddhist philosophy and psychology emphasising the study of cognition, perception, and consciousness through the interior lens of meditative and yogic practices — *L. R.*

[165] I was able to discover that these ideas are attributed to Asanga (4th century C. E.), the founder of the Cittamatra school, as he was interpreted by Je Tsongkhapa in his classical commentary entitled *The Essence of Eloquence* — *L.R.*

East, and of the immense poverty in Africa and Asia? Does this lack of knowledge harm anyone? Does it make people unhappy? Is there someone who will be made happy with this knowledge, or unhappy because of his or her lack of it? Is this knowledge as indispensable as the air we breathe?

The truth is that this lack of knowledge does make people unhappy. This knowledge is in reality as necessary to us as the air we breathe and the water we drink. It is Europe in particular that needs it so much. It is so because it is the European population that became almost insane by following the first extreme. What I say is not just an abstract opinion of a scholar. It is reality.

Now I will try to show you how your failure to understand what emptiness is takes away your freedom and your happiness since your very childhood.

To see how it happens you should remember two terms: Logic and intuition.

What is logic? It is a mental reflection of the real word by means of abstract schemes, figures, or signs we operate. Logic looks like a military leader who models a real battle using small figures of knights, soldiers, elephants, and castles. This is how the game of chess was invented. Most of us use concepts instead of chess figures. Our wooden knights are words and signs. You have to know that a concept is an abstract ideal thing which always follows the rules you or others invented before and which doesn't actually exist in reality. A knight of chess always moves in the same way, however many chess figures there might be on the chessboard. But in reality such knights, such horses had never existed. Logic is a good thing. The trouble begins when we forget that logic simplifies reality. People who use logic forget it all the time.

What is intuition? It is the power of our mind to realise

something by using the very thing we try to understand. To be more exact, not the 'thing,' but the substrate of it. It happens when we look at things, listen to them, taste them — or just realise ideas. Intuition is impossible without six senses.[166]

Now an example. You are cooking a salad. You add salt to it. Then you take a spoon and taste it. You feel it needs improving. So you take a pinch of salt again, add it to your salad anew, taste it again. This is intuition. Now realise that you don't use words while cooking. It is only salt and your tongue you use.

However, when you take a book of recipes and learn from it that you are to add salt to your salad, you are thinking logically. So recipes also list the exact amount of ingredients. So many pinches of salt for a half pound of salad. Words like 'pound' and 'pinch' are just words. There is no such thing as a 'pure' pound. It necessarily is a pound of something. Nonetheless, you trust your book of recipes and add salt to your salad according to its text. It is because you believe that words show things as they are. It is because you are following the first extreme. You do believe that salt exists ultimately, as a source of happiness and health, that salted things are good in themselves. This is how conceptual evaluative thinking appears. You forgot to ask your own body whether salt is good or bad for *you*, though. Your own body surely must be much cleverer than your book of recipes. However, you believe in what others say or write, and you don't trust your body.

I don't ask you to discard logic altogether. Relying only on intuition is like riding a horse instead driving a car. Logic is a good thing, is something airports, cars, and fridges cannot work without. Without logic, you Western people would never invent your clever machines that do much good. But there is too much logic

---

[166] Six senses are five basic senses and cognition of phenomena — *L. R.*

in Western countries, in my opinion. There is only logic in your heads.

It begins as soon as you start going to school.

Take a look at your Western schools. Kids who have just entered it are taught mathematics. Mathematics is the purest essence of logic, it deals only with abstract numbers. Five and five makes ten. Five what? What is the object of this addition? Numbers without their objects never exist in reality. This is a thing you forget to mention when you teach mathematics to your children. Quite the opposite: you persuade them to believe that numbers in themselves are real. That they do exist independently from other things. Everything is made to make a child believe that the concept of a number is as substantial as real things are. Children who don't believe it are punished by schoolteachers and by parents. What is their punishment? Low marks and grades. Marks and grades, it means the same conventional numbers and letters. Those letters and numbers are pure convention. 'A' doesn't necessarily mean 'excellent.' 'A' in itself is just a sound or a letter. However, children were made to believe that marks and grades are real. How can kids help believing that? Their school marks have an impact on the mood of their parents, and this mood is quite a substantial thing for children.

It is a big pity that your Western education system is gradually spreading to India and China. As a result, our Tibetan children are persuaded to believe in essential and real numbers, too. This destroys their mental well-being. You won't succeed to make our children very close-minded, though. Western teachers, schools, and manuals are still in small numbers in Asia. I don't know what comes next. Being uneducated sometimes does good, as you see.

What else are children taught in your schools? Their native language is one of main school subjects. But how is it taught? By making them learn grammar rules. These rules are extremely conventional, they were invented by scholars simply for convenience's sake. There is in fact no incorrect speech at all. All words you utter are correct as long as others understand what you say. Any language is created by men. Nobody will regard a child as 'irregular,' even an imbecile one. Children just differ. In Germany, people often say 'Klaussein,' when they mean that a certain thing belongs to Klaus. They don't say 'Klausens' which is regular and grammatically correct. Logic classifies words like 'Klaussein' as wrong. Intuition tells us that such words simply belong to our everyday language. Everyday language is not wrong. There are times you do need it. For example, while speaking with rude people when you wish to be understood. Or when you wish to get off safe and uninjured from this conversation.

I don't mean that you need to forget grammar rules and become uneducated persons. Rules are of use. They cultivate us, they tame our rudeness. As for me, I don't regard someone who has learnt hundreds of rules as an educated person. I see as a well-educated man someone who has got a feeling for language. Feeling is intuition. But you cannot possibly foster your linguistic feeling if you believe that rules are absolute. Nonetheless, it is exactly absoluteness of rules you were taught in school.

When I arrived in Europe and was studying European languages, I often was corrected, especially by some Germans. Pointing at others' mistakes is a very German feature. I knew only a few German words, so I tried to construct them. I said *gehte*, i.e. 'goed,' instead of *ging*, i.e. 'went,' which is the correct word for the past tense of *gehen*, 'to go.' I said about a tree that the tree *blättert* when I wanted to say that it has leaves, or *Blätter*, whereas the German word *blättern* in fact means 'to turn pages.' It surely was wrong. In Tibetan language you are not bound to rules so much. Our language is somehow softer. In Tibetan, a male disciple may be called *lobpa* as well as *lobma*. *Pa* is a masculine suffix, whereas *ma* is a feminine one. And yet, it is not incorrect to use either of them. To call something in Tibetan, there are many correct variants. I am afraid that after getting in touch with the Western languages, the Tibetan language will become as conservative as they are. Sad it will be! But let us get back to our subject.

I invented new German words and was corrected. Then, having studied German, I began to read some German authors. Nietzsche[167], for example. It is not time to speak about the philosophy of Nietzsche where everything is mixed up, Good with Evil. I simply want to say that I was astonished by Nietzsche's way of using words. He invented new words much in the same way I did. Nobody regards these new words as mistakes. Quite the contrary: everyone says that Nietzsche is a genius, a master of language. He certainly is one, but he would never become one had he been a product of your modern education system where absoluteness of grammar rules as well as their existing independently is proclaimed. No master of language can ever be educated at your schools where conventional rules are made to be idols.

This is true for each school subject also. Consider history. Is history given to children as rough material? Quite the opposite. The rough material of history is ancient manuscripts, laws, documents, poems, and even pictures. Getting in touch with them, the student may feel the character of ages gone. He or she may cultivate his or her intuition this way. A 'polished' history differs from its rough substance. Opinions of researchers constitute the 'easy-made' history. Opinions always rely on concepts, not upon the substrate of history. And above that, there are a great number of terms invented by your scholars in order to simplify history. One should never try to simplify history, though. There are

---

[167] Friedrich Nietzsche was a German philosopher, cultural critic, composer, poet, philologist, and Latin and Greek scholar whose work has exerted a profound influence on modern intellectual history — *L. R.*

terms like 'revolution,' 'capitalism,' 'socialism,' 'communism,' and 'theocracy.' These words are concepts, but the real processes they signify are free of the nature of these concepts. I don't think that the German revolution of 1848[168] was the same as the revolution in Cuba.[169] Theocracy in Tibet was not the same as the state of Vatican in the middle ages. We have never had inquisitors. We have never burnt our magicians alive. There still are a great number of magicians in Tibet. Well, I have just explained why they are so well preserved. We didn't have any crusades. Our wars were not motivated by lamas and monks, our clergy never took part in them. Does it look like any of the European theocracies? But your schoolteachers are very fond of persuading their disciples that such words as 'theocracy' do mean something independently from societies they describe. In fact, schoolboys and schoolgirls are as successful in school as they are capable of *labelling* things. Things that have been already labelled by your scholars. Within their minds, no real work proceeds. As soon as these boys and girls grow up and in their turn become scholars — some of them, I mean — they start debating about the nature of the terms they used in school. They are disputing about what 'revolution' or 'democracy' is. Arguing about words is not very good. The word 'revolution,' like each word, means in fact only what we want it to mean, neither more nor less.

Now consider how the academic performance of schoolboys and schoolgirls is evaluated. Tests. Filling in a form. In those forms, only one answer is to tick off, only one is told to be correct. So a student gets used to the idea that there always *is* a correct answer to *any* question, and that there is only *one* correct answer to any

---

[168] The modern term is 'The German revolutions of 1848–49' — L. R.

[169] The Cuban Revolution was an armed revolt conducted by Fidel Castro's revolutionary 26th of July Movement and its allies against the military dictatorship of Cuban President Fulgencio Batista. The revolution began in July 1953 and continued until the rebels finally ousted Batista on 31 December 1958, replacing his government with a revolutionary socialist state — L. R.

question, discovered by some very clever scientists. The student begins to think that words display reality; that only a professional can find what truth is; and that he or she, the student, is not capable of finding the truth. You know, you cannot *feel* a correct answer when you fill in a test form. You cannot use your intuition. So it fades away, dies off. Words never display reality just by themselves, because each word is merely a concept. It is a sign which is not the same as the thing it displays. And, what is most important, concepts never let us *feel* things. Concepts are empty of the nature of things. This is the fact we must realise very well.

Well, cannot one actually go without intuition? Yes, one can go without. But I want to tell you what going without intuition looks like.

Let us begin with fashion. Fashion, yes. Here in Europe you can hardly find a tastefully dressed woman. You will probably say that you don't care. This is not true. You do. Looking attractive is important for every woman.[170] But your Western women don't believe their own eyes, they don't trust their intuition. Their intuition began to be subdued when they were schoolgirls. It was being subdued for decades and so it died off completely. A Western woman doesn't believe that she is 'professional' enough to design her clothes. There are professional designers and dressmakers who do it better, she thinks. And following the whims of designers your women wear military boots with square toe. Even if I weren't a monk I wouldn't like to live with a woman who wears military boots. I would be afraid of getting under her heel. A third of European women are bringing up their children without assistance of children's father. Half of Western marriages end in divorce. No wonder. On the contrary, you should wonder why some Western children still have fathers.

---

[170] Modern feminists would definitely say it sounds misogynic — *L. R.*

Intuition is the female part of our mind. Logic is its male part. There is a pair called *thab* and *sherab*.[171] The method and the wisdom. Logic is the method, the male part. Intuition is the wisdom, the female part. Your education system kills intuition so it's no wonder your women become manlike. We shouldn't criticise these women. We ought to help them. But helping them is difficult, because their manlike rudeness and their lack of tact combine with their female lack of logic.[172]

I have already told you how to stay healthy. In fact it is just your lack of intuition that causes diseases. Somebody wrote that raw vegetables are very healthy. So everyone now eats them. I, too, probably should do it — this is what you think. You don't care that you personally cannot stand raw vegetables. They have too much of the substrate we Tibetans call 'water' or 'phlegm.' For some people raw vegetables are positively unhealthy. But you keep believing in books, you don't trust your intuition. Little do you care that you shorten your life for five years! You lived this life as science prescribes, and you can boast of it. The idea that you were eating healthy vegetables for so many years surely must console you at the end of your life. You are laughing at our Indian and Tibetan mythology, you regard the Garuda[173] or Sri Devi[174] as a legend, as a fairy-tale, as something nobody has ever seen. But the real legend is your calories nobody has ever seen. However, these legendary calories do shorten the lives of persons who believe in them and keep counting them.

---

[171] The union of wisdom (Sanskrit *prajña*) and method/skillful means (Sanskrit *upaya*) is a very important concept in Tibetan Buddhism. Rinpoche gives their Tibetan names — L. R.

[172] Now, this sounds very misogynistic — L. R.

[173] The *Garuda* is a legendary bird or bird-like creature in Hindu, Buddhist and Jain mythology — L. R.

[174] *Palden Lhamo*, also called Śri Devi, is a protecting deity of the Gelug school of Tibetan Buddhism. She is also the wrathful deity considered to be the principal protectress of Tibet — L. R.

Now some words about your music. You turn on your telly, your computer, or your iPad and listen to modern music. If you ever had so much of intuition as a pinch you would certainly feel how loathsome this music is. But you don't trust your own senses. You believe in words and opinions of your 'professionals,' you trust someone who is a PhD, a scholar, someone who was studying music for ten years. It was not the music by itself he studied, though, but the opinions of other scholars, something they said about music without actually feeling it. And you surely will find your PhD or, maybe, a music performer, it means a person who gets your money by producing the noise you call music. And this PhD or this music performer tells you about something in modern music you 'laypersons' are said never to realise. About deep thoughts it provokes and deep feelings it displays. About its special 'features,' and 'swing,' and whichever words they may use. And you believe him because you are afraid to show your 'ignorance.' In fact, it is your very belief in words that *is* ignorance.

May modern music awaken your intuition? I think not!　　　Intuition must be trained on difficult objects. Intuition is sensitiveness: a fine taste, a keen ear, an observing eye, a sensitive mind. There is nothing in the modern Western music that can train your sensitiveness. This music is as simple as an arithmetic lesson. It is very loud, and its rhythm never changes.

The worst thing happens when someone whose intuition is as good as dead enters religion. It is bad for any religion. For Buddhism it surely is the worst thing we can imagine. A person with underdeveloped intuition ascribes absolute meanings to conventional words and terms. Such a behaviour can never bring one to the Final Liberation. On the contrary, is enslaves us and makes us even less intelligent than we have been.

Now two examples.

There is such a term as *loong*. A *loong* is a Tibetan word which means 'permission' or 'handle.' A handle of a jug, for instance. Receiving a *loong* means that your perception is now, when you have meditated a lot, to some extent changed. It means that now, you can 'hold' it. *Loong* is a concept. Not the loong in itself. The word 'loong.' There is no permission and no perception which exists without the one who perceives. But some Buddhists do believe in transmissions one can 'get' from someone else as if it were a stone or a slice of ham. The only thing needed for it would be a lama who has already 'got' this transmission from another lama. The lama should surely store all the transmissions he has 'got' in a special box. Or in a fridge, like slices of ham, to keep them all right. You cannot 'get' a loong. You only can feel it. Most of Western Buddhists are people with dumb intuition, though. They don't understand what a figurative meaning is. So they seriously ask everyone whether one has 'got' a transmission. I do hope that I am not speaking about people in this prayer hall.

A *lama* is another example. I am often asked whether someone is a qualified lama. If you realised the idea of emptiness you would never ask questions like this one. There is no use of asking another person whether someone is a lama or not. Why asking me? Ask yourselves instead.

A lama is like a mother. This woman is my mother. Does it necessarily mean that she is yours? Must your mother be mine? It probably will be mine, too, if you are my spiritual brother or my spiritual sister. I don't regard all people on earth as my brothers and sisters, though. I should wish it were so. I am not a buddha, you know. I am just a common monk.

A lama is a 'thing.' There are two parts of each thing: the substrate and the name. The substrate of a lama is a person who starts doing what lamas usually do. Then someone else comes and calls this person a lama. In this moment a 'lama' appears. For whom is he a lama? For someone who calls him so. There will be another 'thing' for another person. No lama. You surely cannot call everybody a lama. The substrate of a thing must roughly correspond to its name, if only a bit. You can sharpen a knife with a stone. A shingle can hardly be used as a grindstone, though. So the name must correspond to its substrate. But it depends on the perception on the name-giver whether it corresponds and how much it corresponds. We usually see in the outer world something that is our own nature. When an angel, a man, and a demon look at a glass of water, the angel sees it as ambrosia, the man perceives is as water, the demon finds it to be urine or blood. Both ambrosia and urine are real. It doesn't mean that each lama is an illusion. Neither does it mean that there are no lamas at all, nor that everyone might be a lama. It only means that a 'lama' appears when we give the title of a lama to a person. Imagine that I go for a walk in lay clothes. That I cross a street without regard to traffic lights. That I am caught by a policeman. A lama ceases to exist then. A petty criminal appears.

Look at the lamp under the ceiling. Now put your finger before your eyes. How many lamps do you see? Two.[175] How many exist in reality? Two. I am not joking. Your logic says that there cannot possibly be two lamps. But is it your logic or your intuition you trust? If you had two eyes, a human and a dog's one, you couldn't see colours by one of your eyes. You would see two lamps then, a yellow lamp and a grey one.[176] There would be two lamps for you. There are no yellow lamps in the world of dogs. Only the grey ones. And these grey lamps are as real as yellow ones.

---

[175] What Rinpoche describes happens as long as we focus our sight on the finger rather than on the lamp. This evidently has to do with the fact that each of our eyes transmits a slightly different image to the brain, which the brain then interprets as a single image. — *L. R.*

[176] Which is probably wrong, as modern researches prove that dogs can perceive yellow — *L. R.*

I am expected to award 'lama's certificates'. I try to avoid it, though. If you believed in your intuition, not in papers, you wouldn't need them. Clothes and food that I like may be unhealthy for someone else. Also a teaching given by a person I believe to be a lama might do harm to another person, someone who is not like me. But how can you Europeans trust your intuition if you have never used it? You have less intuition than a child. How long should you cultivate it before you really can use it! Religious life without intuition looks like driving a car with shut eyes. Well, not a car: you probably can drive a car by means of your logic. It is like riding a horse. Someone who rides a horse thinking it is a machine, someone who doesn't care what the horse feels will fall down from its back. I don't mean knights, the wooden horses of chess. Those wooden horses always move in the same way. The behaviour of a real horse depends both on what it feels and on what its rider also feels. Well if you only hurt yourself after falling down from a horse. You may break your neck as well. Religion is like riding a horse. Religion is a real living being. This is why no absolute unmistakable way of achieving Liberation has ever existed. There are some rules which might be of use for you. But the real religious life is much more difficult than those rules. Breaking a conventional rule is sometimes better than falling down from the back of your religion.

You shouldn't think that religious rules are of no use at all. Thinking like this is another extreme. It is wrong to think that each thing is conventional, even things like suffering, human virtues, or Liberation. Nothing is substantial, then. Then you are wasting time sitting here. Then you do not need to live at all. There is no difference for you *'to be or not to be,'* then. This is the extreme we Asian people usually fall into. You Western people seldom do it. There also are some individuals who follow two extremes at once. I would never believe it if I didn't see them with my own eyes.

There are some narrow paths in Tibetan mountains. Sometimes you find human bones and skulls when walking on them. There are a good number of corpses of persons that have fallen down from the back of religion. Their corpses lie on the narrow path of

the European Buddhism. I am not going to increase this number. But it doesn't depend only on me.

What do you need to stay on the back of the horse of the Dharma, not to fall down, not to injure yourself? To begin with, stop believing in words and their absolute meaning. Stop doing what you have been doing till now. The most dangerous words to believe in their absolute meaning are such Buddhist terms as *bodhisattva*, *bodhicitta*, *Liberation*, *paramita*, and the like. Never, never should you believe that things these words label exist in their own way, without relying on our perception. These terms just attempt to point at the substrate they are linked with. So you ought to learn the very nature of bodhicitta and Liberation instead of learning words. It will be hard for you after many years spent without practice. It will be as difficult for you as to start walking for someone who couldn't walk for ten years. The substrate of religion is the most difficult thing to perceive: it is easy to see a tree, but seeing a bodhisattva of wisdom is much more difficult. Seeing is not imagining things, this is what I want to emphasise.

I hope all of you understand how important this seeing is. I hope that you will walk. I hope that you will be able to explain to others how to walk. I hope that you can walk without using words as your feet. The feet you need are quite different. It is the feet of your senses and of your mind you need.

Buddhism and Christianity

When the king Suddhodana, the Buddha's father, wanted to start a war with another king, the Enlightened One appeared with His Sangha and stayed in a forest between two armies. No battle followed. The Buddha was very far from being a politician. However, in that case He influenced the political life of India. Was it only a weakness, inspired by sight of His old father? I don't think so. Tathagatas have no weaknesses. The One Thus Gone showed us by this act that we must struggle against Evil by different means, sometimes by 'worldly' actions, too. We must work not only on our own mind, but also on the world we live in.

The same idea was taught by Jesus whom Christians worship as a god.[177] Jesus whom we Buddhists also may call a bodhisattva for His great compassion. Now the followers of Christ realise this idea much better than we Buddhists do. They may have never realised other ideas of Him. They may have never understood anything in Jesus' Teaching but this very idea. It may be. However, they have realised this one.

Check it out for yourself. American and European highways, cars, phones, computers, central heating, and washing machines – everything like this is a result of their efforts to make the world a better place to live in. You may tell me that the world never becomes better by producing cars and washing machines. But in fact you mix up two things, the world and the man. The man doesn't become better by producing or using washing machines. The world does. When I was young we washed clothes by hand. I would be very glad to get a washing machine at that time, even

---

[177] It is very difficult to explain the difference between 'a god' and 'the God' to any Buddhist. In private conversations, Rinpoche rejected the idea of the Personified God because of philosophical reasons — *L. R.*

an old one. Most Tibetan peasants still have none. Even if they got one, where would they plug it in? Things never make us happier, that's true. But it's also true that some things *do* make our live easier so that we get some more spare time for religious practices. You can hardly find a half of an hour for a meditation if you do your hard work for fourteen hours a day in order to earn your living and not to starve.

Here is one more example. There were so-called *inquisitors* among Christian monks at the time of the Middle Ages, here in Europe. Those monks wanted to 'defeat the devil in the human mind.' Methods they used to defeat the devil were horrible. In some few centuries they had burnt thousands of young women and girls at the stake. It was terrible. Our natural horror and disgust prevent us from realising another simple fact. The fact that some of those monks sincerely *wanted to improve* and to educate people they punished and burnt. They wanted to improve everybody, old and young, each layman and laywoman, to save them from the devil's paws, so to say. The inquisitors had never succeeded in doing that, of course. Having tortured guiltless laymen, they went to hell immediately after their death. But *our* monks have never aimed at a goal like this one. Our Buddhist monks never wanted to save from hell each layman in their country. Was it out of our profound knowledge of human nature? Or just out of laziness? So you can call us both wise enough and coward enough.

When a new religion appears its first mass followers also emerge, its first apostles, so to say. They are good-natured men, as a rule, but no great saints. The destiny of a religion depends on the power of their minds. Even saintly people are not always intelligent. Methinks some religions never came to their blossom because their first apostles were not clever enough. Even the Buddha didn't reveal everything He had realised to His first disciples. Some deep ideas, those of *Prajña Paramita*, He revealed only to the nagas. And they transmitted them to us when we grew mature enough to understand this knowledge.[178] What if some truths He realised are so deep that the nagas keep them hidden from us even now? What if even the nagas were *not* intelligent enough to learn everything He had realised? What if there could be four or five turnings of the Wheel of the Dharma, not only three?[179] What if being ready to turn the Wheel for the fourth time the Buddha saw no one able to comprehend the wisdom of this turn?

Now I want to put a very serious question which some of you will find to be almost blasphemous. The question is as follows: has Buddhism really succeeded as a religion?[180]

Buddhism is a great religion, doubtlessly. Without Buddhism, the whole of Asia would perish in hatred, ignorance, and fanaticism. Buddhism has succeeded, of course. But to what extent has it succeeded? And what shall we call Buddhism?

There are two Tibetan terms both of which mean and can be translated as 'Buddhism' into English. The first is *sangye kyi cho*, or 'the Buddha's Teaching.' The last is *nangcho*, or 'our inner tradition.'

Now I tell you that *sangye kyi cho* is not the same as *nangcho*. The former is much deeper, much wider, and much more difficult. We are not able to learn the whole Truth, as it was realised by the Buddha Himself. Maybe only the nagas can understand it in its unthinkable complexity. Maybe even they cannot. I think they cannot. If a certain naga reached Enlightenment and became a buddha, his glory would spread upon the whole world, upon

---

[178] This is a popular Tibetan belief explaining how the so-called *terma* texts, or 'hidden scriptures', came into existence — L. R.

[179] The fact that some Buddhist tenets are in fact contradictory is usually explained by means of the 'three turnings of the Wheel', i.e. three different ways to teach the Dharma, each of them is said to be more profound than the previous one — L. R.

[180] A breathtaking question. Something you never expect from a Buddhist teacher — L. R.

the whole Universe, because even the nagas learnt about the Buddha after His Enlightenment. But how can one realise what the Buddha had realised without becoming oneself a buddha? It lets me think that even the nagas didn't understand completely what the Buddha really told them. And how can we know that He told them everything He knew?

You should ask me why it is so important. It is so important because it means that our 'Buddhism,' our *nangcho* we use and practise is not very good. It is not bad. It is useful for personal liberation. But it is not *completely* good. This incompleteness is not the Buddha's fault. It's ours.

You may think that religion is something like cooked turnip Je Tsongkhapa wrote about in the first volume of *Lamrimchenmo*[181]. Be it good or bad, fresh or old, a hungry person eats it anyway, and it helps him or her not to starve. You are mistaken if you think so. There is a certain grade, a certain point on the way of degrading. Having passed beyond this point, a religion becomes a poison. One day a very old broth will be poisonous, too.[182]

Let us consider the following historical facts.

I have been spending much time studying the history of Europe. In the twentieth century, Europe took part in two terrible world wars. World War II was not only a struggle between several armies. It was a great battle between two traditions, between *marpoi ringlug* and *phashisi ringlug*, between communism and the

---

[181] 'Once, there were some children there who, being hungry and wishing to eat roasted barley flour, asked their mother for food. Since she had no roasted barley flour, she offered them fresh turnip, which they refused. Then she offered them dried turnip, but they did not want that either, so she then gave them cooked turnip. But they turned this down as well. Finally she offered them frozen cooked turnip, whereupon they turned away with a great feeling of nausea, exclaiming, "Everything is turnips!"'(Tsongkhapa. *The Great Treatise on the Stages of the Path to Enlightenment*. New York: Snow Lion Publications, 2000.) — L.R.

[182] This happens because food-borne bacteria multiply over time — L. R.

German national-socialism, or fascism. The Germans dislike the word 'fascism.' Preposterous,[183] isn't it? They are like a murderer who insists on the title of 'killer' for himself. For me, there is not much difference between a murderer and a killer.

In Tibetan, the word 'lug' stands for a religious tradition, too. A normal member of a political movement never worships

his or her leader as a god. If he or she does, there is no politics more. There is a new religion.

Both fascism and communism had their followers, their practitioners, their rituals, their lamas, even their living deities. Their leaders were both cruel tyrants, but this is not the point I wish to emphasise. Having meditated on both of them we realise that the German fascism was a degraded form of our 'inner tradition,' *nangcho*, as well as the Russian communism was a perverse variant of Christianity.[184]

First of all, look at their symbols. As you know, the swastika was the symbol of the German national socialism. I think there is no need to explain that the swastika is a Buddhist symbol, that of the Dharma Wheel.[185] The symbols of the communism were a star and the *zorathoba:* the sickle-and-hammer. Now recall that when Jewish astrologers[186] saw a new star on the sky they knew that Jesus was born. A sickle is used to cut wheat. There is no bread without wheat. There is no Christianity without bread. The bread symbolises *corpus Christi*, the body of Jesus. Jesus got in touch with a hammer at the beginning and at the very end of

---

[183] I think Rinpoche said 'funny'. I replaced it by 'preposterous' as, after all, there is nothing even remotely amusing in fascism — *L. R.*

[184] A very paradoxical conclusion, unorthodox for both Christians and Buddhists — *L. R.*

[185] The swastika was a Hindu and a Buddhist symbol long before the Nazi party started to use it as its emblem — *L. R.*

[186] Rinpoche refers to the biblical Magi (see Matthew 2:1-12), also called the Three Wise Men or Three Kings, who definitely were not Jewish — *L. R.*

His life. He used a hammer when He worked as a carpenter. And He was nailed to His cross by a hammer, too. In fact, the communist sickle and hammer form a cross, the main Christian symbol.[187]

You should recall, secondly, that Adolf Hitler sent some expeditions to Tibet. He even brought some Tibetan lamas to Germany. Those lamas could be only magicians of the Bön tradition,[188] not real lamas. And they were brought not to teach the Dharma, of course. Adolf Hitler just wanted to learn how to manipulate people, I suppose. However, he looked for Tibetan lamas, not for Christian monks.

Very important is the character of the persons the national-socialists and the communists used to worship. The former developed the ideal of a hero, of an *Übermensch*, i. e. of a superman who may dare something common people never dare. Such a hero should be an *Arier*, which is a German word for an *arya*,[189] and could be identified through certain 'physical signs' like colour of his hair. Is it not a corrupted Buddhist idea? *'A true Brahmana goes scatheless, though he has killed father and mother, and two valiant kings, though he has destroyed a kingdom with all its subject'*, the Dhammapada says[190]. This doesn't mean that an *arhat*[191] can kill his mother and his father. An arhat never kills a single worm.

---

[187] These parallels between Buddhism and Nazism, and between Christianity and Communism are of course very doubtful. On the other hand, they reveal Rinpoche as someone who was never afraid to explore problematic issues — L. R.

[188] Bon also spelled Bön, is the native Tibetan folk religion. It is characterised by Animism, Shamanism and ancestor worship — L. R.

[189] An *arya* in Buddhism is a 'noble one', a saint man — L. R.

[190] Another translation has it as follows: 'Having slain mother and father / And two khattiya kings, / Having slain a kingdom together with the subordinate, / Without trembling, the brahmana goes' (The Dhammapada. Ch. XXI, V. 294. Translated by John Ross Carter and Mahinda Palihawadana. New York: Oxford University Press, 2000). Normally it is interpreted as 'killing' one's own obscurations and destroying their 'kingdom' in one's mind — L. R.

[191] Arhat is defined in Theravada Buddhism as one who has gained insight into the true nature of existence and has achieved Nirvana – L. R.

Sayings like the one I have just quoted are very dangerous. Do you know that   arhats are also called aryas, i. e. 'the noble ones'? In any case, you certainly know that every buddha has got thirty-two great and eighty small *laksanas*, i. e. physical signs. And he surely possesses some supernatural powers, those of a 'superman.'

The communists didn't worship supermen. It was martyrs they admired. During World War I their martyrs were persecuted by 'capitalists,' during World War II — by German national-socialists, by 'supermen.' They were persecuted and tortured, but they always kept believing in their leader, their semi-god. And even this deity, their first leader, Vladimir Lenin,[192] in their eye was a 'martyr,' like Jesus.[193] He died from a serious malady, having been injured by his political enemies. No communist could become well-known after his death without being tortured by his enemies.[194] No religion counts more martyrs than communism does. No one but Christianity.

The ideas are most important. It is difficult for me to tell the main idea of the German national socialism. I only know its slogan *'Arbeit macht frei,'* 'Your efforts liberate you,' written on the gates of the concentration lager in Auschwitz. It is a cynical saying when written on the gates of a prison nobody could escape from. Yet it is a Buddhist one, if we think that the Buddha reached Enlightenment only by His own efforts, without being helped by deities. In fact, the national socialists wished more *Lebensraum*[195], more 'space for living.' They wanted to break their cage, not 'the steel cage of passions', but the cage of their state borders. Like us

---

[192] Vladimir Ulyanov (1870 – 1924), better known by his alias Lenin, was a Russian revolutionary, politician, and political theorist. He served as head of government of Soviet Russia from 1917 to 1922 and of the Soviet Union from 1922 to 1924 — *L. R.*

[193] Which fact doesn't, of course, allow us to call him a real martyr — *L. R.*

[194] A doubtful statement — *L. R.*

[195] The German concept of *Lebensraum* (German 'living space') comprises policies and practices of settler colonialism which proliferated in Germany from the 1890s to the 1940s — *L. R.*

Buddhist monks they attacked and killed their 'inner enemies.' Not obscurations, of course. The Jews.

Do you know the main belief of communists? It was their belief in communism. To say it in other words, they believed that once, by collective efforts of the whole of mankind, the world will become beautiful so that everybody in this world will be happy. This is a Christian idea that I have already told you about. I don't mean by 'Christian' its exclusive belonging to Jesus' Teaching, *yeshui cho.* I mean its being part of the European Christian tradition, *chiling kyi cholug,* but not a part of *nangcho.*

I guess nobody dares now proclaim that each reflection of the Buddha's Teaching is still 'eatable,' even such a corrupt one as *phashisi ringlug*[196]. There are some [Buddhist] monks here, and they may be now insulted when they hear that I compare Buddhism with the German national socialism. They will proclaim that we Buddhists have nothing in common with fascists. Of course we don't. And yet, who can determine with certainty how far the actual Buddhism, *nangcho,* is from the genuine Teaching of the Buddha, *sangye kyi cho*? What if Buddhism is as bad a caricature of the real Truths discovered by the Buddha as national socialism is a caricature of Buddhism? I am not a buddha, so I am not able to determine it.

There is another important thing. In the struggle between communism and national socialism, the former won. Maybe because it was a bit better as a 'turnip broth,' as a religion for the hungry mankind. It was a very small bit better, but this 'bit' was enough.

Now I ask you to forget the idea of tolerance and that one of the equal value of different religions. They are true, but also false. Everyone here is close to me so you can understand me, hopefully. Listen attentively.

---

[196] Tibetan for fascism — *L. R.*

Buddhism is better than Christianity in some respects. (I mean the now existing 'Buddhism' and 'Christianity,' the *nangcho* and *chiling kyi cholug*, not the Teachings of the Buddha or Christ *in themselves*.) It is more intelligent. More tolerant. More peaceful. More useful for a personal practice, because it describes many skillful means of getting enlightened and requires no mediation of priests when using these means. It doesn't inspire fanaticism and exaggerated hopes, as a rule.[197] Buddhism is better in many respects but one. It doesn't wish to improve this suffering world. It only suggests escaping from samsara. By doing so, it rejects the Buddha who influenced politicians rather than avoid politics altogether. And this one aspect of Buddhism may be worse than all disadvantages of Christianity.[198]

Morality in Christian countries fades away. Not more than one person of a hundred is here a monk or a serious practitioner. In Tibet, the religion is still alive, the faith is still strong there. Before the Chinese invasion, one third of our population might be monks.

However, each layman in Western countries now has an opportunity to practise religion, because he or she has enough spare time for spiritual activities.

A peasant in Tibet has no such opportunity. An uneducated peasant in Tibet, India, or Vietnam has neither free time nor necessary knowledge of how he or she should work on his or her mind. The more he or she studies the Dharma the less time he or she has left for his or her job, the worse he or she lives. We Tibetans had produced the greatest philosophy. In the third volume of *Lamrimchenmo*, hundreds of pages are devoted to an interdependent existence of a *shingta khorlo*, a carriage. However, until

---

[197] All these statements are, of course, either naïve or slightly prejudiced and can be contradicted by Christians — L. R.

[198] This famous and dumbfounding conclusion led some of Rinpoche's critics so far as to call him a 'hidden Christian' which he, of course, wasn't — L. R.

the Chinese invasion we had no carriages at all. Our well-educated monks had no interest in constructing carriages, because 'carriages are interdependent and don't exist ultimately.' The monastic life is pure and good, but there is no way for everybody to become a monk. This is our old Tibetan division in 'aryas,' the supermen, and the common people, metaphorically speaking, the Jews who shall die in the concentration lager of samsara. We aryas, like the German *Ariers*, always say, 'Your efforts liberate you,' yet we know that their working hard won't liberate them. We Tibetans didn't invent bombs and machine guns. But neither have we invented a carriage or a washing machine. Someone can regard washing clothes by hand as a spiritual training, to be sure. But for most people, it is still washing clothes by hand.

What has a good Buddhist to do if he or she realises this big fault of his or her inner tradition? Must he or she become a Christian? Of course not. There is one thing a Buddhist can do, though. He or she should meditate upon the ways to make this world a better place. It is not always a big task like building a school or a hospital. Helping one's own old relatives or ill people will do, too. The Buddha taught an active compassion that improves this world by action, not only by meditation. We don't seem to understand this teaching yet. This ignorance is not the Buddha's fault. It's ours.

Four Truths

There is probably nothing more important in our Teaching than the Four Noble Truths. There is probably nothing more profound in our canon than the sutras of the Perfection of Wisdom, or *Prajña Paramita*. The *Prajña Paramita Hridaya Sutra* is said to be the very essence, the 'heart' of the Perfection of Wisdom. Surely everyone is eager to know how the most important ideas of Buddhism are described in the most profound Mahayana sutra. Do you want to know it, too? Here it is.

Deshindu dugngalwa dang
kuenjungwa dang
gogpa dang
lam me.

The meaning of these words is as follows:

there is no suffering,
no source of suffering,
no end of suffering,
no Path.

These words seem to be easy, but it is a heavy task to understand them properly.

Let us begin with the First Truth. *There is no suffering.*

You may imagine it means that there is no suffering at all. There are two extremes one is inclined to fall into while meditating on these words. It is you people of the West who do think there is no suffering. You live exactly this way. You never care too much about your health or about your death that is sure to come. You regard suffering as something shameful. You are afraid to be told to suffer. One who suffers cannot be successful, cannot work properly and so one loses everything one has earned before. This is precisely so in your cruel Western world. However, one who carefully avoids suffering is never able to escape from samsara. What will he or she escape from? What will be his or her motivation?

Some of you think more deeply. Some religious people in the Western countries are able to face suffering. They claim that this very suffering is joy. Each time you feel pain you have to *enjoy* it. This Christian idea is profound. And yet, it is perfectly useless for an average person. To feel joy instead of pain, one must first cultivate one's own mind for a very long time. Some of you attempt to do it without the necessary training. Having failed, they immediately begin to regard their own religion as a collection of old lies. I, a Buddhist, think it is more than just that.

We people of the East fall into another extreme. We understand the words of the Buddha too directly. We realise very well that there is much suffering in the world. So why should one care about worldly affairs if there is nothing but suffering? Suffering exists once for all. Nobody can change it. Building schools, hospitals, creating new machines is of no use, because no effort can ever destroy this huge amount of suffering. This is what we Asian people think. So we drop it altogether. We prefer dreams to real deeds. I cannot say which extreme is worse. Both are quite bad.

Is there any suffering, or is there none, then? Suffering surely exists. And yet, it has never existed by its own way, relying on itself. There is no substance of suffering in the world. There really are the substances of earth, water, air, and fire in the Universe. But no real substance of independent suffering has ever existed, nor could there be any. The only substance of it is our mind. It is quite wrong to say, 'Suffering exists.' Say instead, 'Suffering *beings* exist.' This is much better. This probably will prevent you from your indifference towards the world we people of the East suffer from. This probably will awaken in you an active compassion towards suffering beings we people of the East lack so much.

Imagine that all beings living on earth simultaneously disappear. The thing called 'the earth' will disappear, too, as there will be no one who will be able to call it so. The very matter, the substance of the earth will be still there. But any suffering will cease once for all, as nobody will suffer. This is the reason why no suffering exists independently, in an ultimate way.

What is the origin of suffering? It is our ability to estimate things, to consider them 'bad' or 'good.' As soon as we call a thing 'bad' suffering appears. Imagine a very rich man who suddenly becomes poor. So he is forced to rent a very cheap flat. Only one room, maybe, with only two windows, a table, and a sofa. As soon as he enters the room he calls it 'bad' and suffers. Now imagine a prisoner who gets this room after being discharged from his small and stinky prison cell. How will he enjoy it! Why, in a prison cell he had no sofa and no windows at all. The room is the same in both cases. Our suffering doesn't depend on things around us, as you see. It doesn't even depend on our perception, because both persons see the same two windows. It only depends on our ability to call things 'bad' and to suffer from their being 'bad.'

What lets us call them bad, then? Our ignorance. Ignorance is known as the only origin of suffering. What is ignorance? It is the false idea that things exist independently, that they can be 'good' or 'bad' separately from our mind. Where does this idea spring from? From our self. If a 'self' exists, then outer things exist, too, so we think. In reality, there is only our own mind that we see. The substance of things does exist, but it is our mind that transforms this substance into what we see. However it may be, we cannot help believing in a 'self'. Even some animals have a conception of 'self,' the more we human beings. Without this conception, we would not care for ourselves and thus we would die in a day or two. This is why the *Hridaya Sutra* says there is no origin of suffering. It means that there is no *independent* origin of suffering. This source is not somewhere, like a source of water in a desert. This source is our selves. It is we. This is how you should understand the Second Truth.

I think, too, that it is quite unnecessary to speak about 'belief in independent existence of things being the source of suffering.' The idea is perfectly true. And yet, it has been so often misunderstood, especially by beginners. Having understood it too literally, one can fancy that nothing is easier than Liberation, that to achieve it, one has nothing to do but to realise that the belief in independent existence of things is wrong, and that having grasped that, one gets enlightened in an instant. Nothing could be further from the truth. You cannot get rid of the belief in outer sources of happiness simply by rejecting a philosophical concept, however intelligent you might be. Your mind is much wider than your reason. It is not your reason, but your habits of perception which matter. The more cultivated your habits the less you suffer. And you cannot get good habits without cultivating the six virtues, or, more exactly, the six perfections.

Consider the perfection of giving. Imagine someone who is accustomed to give to others anything one has got. Such a person won't regard his or her property as 'good.' So he or she won't suffer in case something is stolen from him or her or taken away from him or her by force.

Consider the perfection of discipline. A disciplined person is accustomed to obey rules. He or she won't regard even the strictest rules as 'bad.' Such a person won't suffer in a prison, in the army, or wherever strict rules are of necessity.

Consider the perfection of patience. Someone who is accustomed to be patient won't regard physical or mental pain as a very bad thing. So he or she won't suffer much when other people do.

Consider the perfection of enthusiasm. Someone who is accustomed to work hard won't regard labour as 'bad,' so he or she won't suffer from much work.

At last, consider the perfections of concentration and wisdom. Someone who is able to concentrate and analyse thoroughly can easily learn new things. Such a person can easily cultivate other perfections, and thus escape from suffering. Moreover, a wise person can even realise that our happiness relies only on our mind. A simple understanding of this fact is still not enough to achieve Liberation, but it lessens our suffering and makes the roots of other virtues stronger.

There is in fact no other way to achieve the Ultimate Freedom but the six perfections. You may ridicule me and think it is only my belonging to the *Gelugpa* school that lets me proclaim it. Think whatever you want. I still believe that no religion can lead a person to Liberation except through cultivating the six perfections. It is precisely so. And why is it so? It is because without perfections one doesn't have the necessary ability to regard 'unpleasant' things as good ones and stay happy with them. This ability doesn't spring simply from belief. This ability is the same as the habit of perception. Imagine that you were robbed. You may sincerely believe that one should be generous. You may repeat it to yourself a hundred times. Yet it won't help you. You will feel unhappy being robbed all the same, if you are not really generous and altruistic. The only way of becoming generous is your generous deeds. There is a law of karma according to which we truly believe something to be good only in case we repeatedly do or choose this something by our own free will. In case we exercise bad deeds we start believing them to be good. Why, it is easy: we cannot help appreciating something we work on. Otherwise it would mean that we work on something we don't need at all. Nobody wants to regard oneself as such an idiot. We believe giving our property away to be good only in case we make donations. We believe discipline to be good only in case we discipline ourselves. We believe endurance of pain to be good only if we exercise in it. We believe labour to be good only if we work hard. And so on, and so on. Without these beliefs, we will feel unhappy each time we feel pain, are robbed, forced to keep some rules, or bound to work hard. You see, there is absolutely no way to Liberation except through perfections, and there is no way to perfections except through good deeds and thoughts.

Now let us proceed to the Third Noble Truth, as it is stated in the *Hridaya Sutra*. 'There is no Liberation.'

Enlightenment surely exists. Nobody would make efforts to achieve something that isn't there. So why is it said that there is no Nirvana? It is so because most of you have a totally wrong conception of Nirvana. Nirvana is not a place you can go. Neither is it some subtle substance heavenly castles are made from. Nirvana is only *the way we see things*. A common person sees things in quite a wrong way. One's personal desire for something obscures the right perception of this thing. You will never see, for instant, what women really are, if you desire them. As soon as you give up your desire for women you learn a great deal about them. Instead of objects of your lust, you see human beings in them. Each monk can be a perfect seducer, you know, for he knows women. He is a bad monk if he does not. And he knows women because he has given up his desire for them. As soon as you have given up all your desires and have cultivated all your perfections to their utmost, you aren't able to perceive any particular thing as something 'bad.' Or, to say it in other words, you see the world as it is. Your mind through which you see the world and the real world that exists don't differ any longer. This is Nirvana. There is no other Nirvana but this very world we live in. And the other way around: there is nothing in this world that doesn't have the nature of Nirvana. This is why no separate Nirvana has ever existed. This is how you should understand the Third Truth.

And now the last Noble Truth comes: that of the Path. 'There is no Path,' the *Hridaya Sutra* says. What is the meaning of this obscure line?

The Path cannot help existing. There is no Liberation without the Path. But what is the Path in itself? Why, you were told it by the Buddha. Correct knowledge, correct deeds, correct speech, correct thoughts, a correct way to earn money, correct efforts, correct attention, and correct concentration. What deeds may be called correct, though? Why, those and only those that form our good habits, those that cultivate our perfections. No particular deed can be considered good or bad once for all. Giving alms to poor people is good. It is bad, however, if you do it out of pride. It is also bad in case you give them your last farthing so that your family has nothing to live with. Murder is bad. Killing a dangerous terrorist is good, though, if you have no other way to stop him. In short, those deeds, words, and thoughts are good that lessen the amount of suffering of all living beings. But these deeds, words, and thoughts are the same deeds, words, and thoughts that we do, say, and think in our everyday life. There are no special religious 'Buddhist' deeds, words, and thoughts. The attention you give to your body and mind while meditating is the same attention you use when crossing a street. It is not a special kind of religious attention. The concentration on the Buddha is the same you use when reading a newspaper. And so on. No separate Path has ever existed. You Western Buddhists imagine the Path to be an American highway with road signs. Now imagine a desert or a field. In a desert, you can go in all directions. There is only one direction which leads to Nirvana. But the field is always the same. There are neither road signs nor asphalt roads in the field of your life, nor can there be any. Spiritual activity is not marked with miraculous signs. Not at the very beginning of your journey, at least. The Path is only a direction in which you are to go. It exists nowhere. It is neither on earth nor in the sky. The direction is all the same for all religions. There cannot be another one. There is no Path separate from life. There is no Buddhist Path separate from the Christian one. Do you really think that Christians can go without cultivating perfections or doing good deeds on their way to their Kingdom of Heaven? You are seriously mistaken if you think so. There is no way of feeling happy and avoiding suffering without perfections. The only thing that distinguishes us Buddhists from Christians is *vahana*, the vehicle. It is the vehicle and not the Path that differs. We Tibetans ride on the back of meditation. Most of Christians go by the bus of communion. Both vehicles can be easily broken by your ignorance, and then you start to believe you are still moving, much in the same way a child plays with a toy bus. Some few Christians may have other vehicles, too. The belief that there are different paths does much harm. It leads to everlasting disputes whose path is better. And more than that: it awfully obscures the way to Liberation. Having decided for yourselves, that the Path exists as an independent entity, you keep looking for asphalt, for a ready-made receipt to make you happy and to destroy all suffering. There are no such receipts! It is only your life that exists. It depends only on you in what direction you go through your life.

Now, as a conclusion, I should repeat the Four Noble Truths, as they are stated in the *Hridaya Sutra*.

There is no suffering. There are suffering beings.
There is no separate source of suffering. Our selves are the source.
There is no Nirvana but the world we live in.
There is no Path but direction.

Think these lines over and over again.

དེ་བཞིན་དུ་སྡུག་བསྔལ་བ་དང་།

ཀུན་འབྱུང་བ་དང་།

འགོག་པ་དང་།

ལམ་མེད།

There is no suffering,

no source of suffering,

no end of suffering,

no Path.